MASTERING
ANGER AND
AGGRESSION
The
Brazelton Way

MASTERING ANGER AND AGGRESSION

The
Brazelton Way

T. Berry Brazelton, M.D.
Joshua D. Sparrow, M.D.

A Merloyd Lawrence Book

DA CAPO LIFELONG BOOKS
A Member of the Perseus Books Group

PHOTO CREDITS
Photographs on pp. iv top right, 70 by Michel Egron-Polak (megron@noos.fr)
Photograph on p. iv bottom left by Dorothy Littell Greco
Photographs on pp. iv top left and bottom right, xx, 14 by Marilyn Nolt
(noltphotos@mail.com)

Text design by Trish Wilkinson
Set in 11-point Adobe Garamond by the Perseus Books Group

Library of Congress Cataloging-in-Publication Data
Brazelton, T. Berry, 1918-
    Mastering anger and aggression the Brazelton way / T. Berry Brazelton, Joshua D.
Sparrow.— 1st Da Capo Press ed.
        p.   cm.
    "A Merloyd Lawrence book."
    Includes bibliographical references and index.
    ISBN 0-7382-1006-4 (pbk. : alk. paper) 1. Anger in children. 2. Child rearing.
3. Child development. 4. Parenting. I. Sparrow, Joshua D. II. Title.
BF723.A4B73 2005
155.4'1247—dc22   2005002359

First Da Capo Press edition 2005

Published by Da Capo Press
A Member of the Perseus Books Group
www.dacapopress.com

Da Capo Press books are available at special discounts for bulk purchases in the U.S.
by corporations, institutions, and other organizations. For more information, please
contact the Special Markets Department at the Perseus Books Group, 11 Cambridge
Center, Cambridge, MA 02142, or call (800) 255-1514 or (617) 252-5298, or e-mail
special.markets@perseusbooks.com.

To the children and parents
who have taught us so much through the years

Contents

Acknowledgments

We would like to thank parents across the country for having first urged us to write these concise, accessible books on topics of the utmost importance to them, for without their vision they might never have been written. Thanks, too, go to Karin Ajmani, Geoffrey Canada, Marilyn Joseph and the Baby College staff, Karen Lawson and her late husband Bart, David Saltzman, and Caressa Singleton for their unwavering support for our work, and from whom we have learned so much. Special thanks go to Ivor Edmonds for his invaluable insights on self-defense for young children. As always we would again like to thank our editor, Merloyd Lawrence, for her wisdom and guidance. Finally, we wish to express our gratitude to our families, not only for their encouragement and patience, but for the lessons they have taught us that we have sought to impart in this book.

Preface

Ever since I wrote the first *Touchpoints* book, published in 1992, I have been asked by parents and professionals all over the country to write some short, practical books on the common challenges that parents face as they raise their children. Among the most common are crying, discipline, sleep, toilet training, feeding, sibling rivalry, and aggression.

In my years of pediatric practice, families have taught me that problems in these areas often arise predictably as a child develops. In these short books I have tried to address the problems that parents are bound to encounter as their children regress just before they make their next developmental leap. Each book describes these "touchpoints"—of crying, discipline, sleep, toilet training, feeding, sibling rivalry, and aggression— so that parents can better understand their child's behavior. Each also offers specific suggestions on how parents can help their child master the challenges they face in these areas so that they can get back on track.

In general these books focus on the challenges of the first six years of life, though occasionally older children's issues are referred to. In the final section, special problems are discussed, though these short books are not intended to cover these topics exhaustively. Instead, we hope that these books will serve as easy-to-use guides for parents to turn to as they face their child's growing pains, or "touchpoints" that signal exciting leaps of development.

As with *Touchpoints Three to Six*, I have invited Joshua Sparrow, MD, to co-author these books with me, to add his perspective as a child psychiatrist. Though difficulties such as temper tantrums, fighting, and biting, for example, are both common and predictable, they make great demands on parents. These kinds of problems are for the most part temporary and not serious, yet without support and understanding, they can overwhelm a family, and send a child's development seriously off course. It is our hope that the straightforward information provided in these books will help prevent those unnecessary derailments, and provide reassurance for parents in times of uncertainty, so that the excitement and joy of helping a young child grow can be rekindled.

MASTERING
ANGER AND
AGGRESSION
The
Brazelton Way

CHAPTER 1

Helping Young Children Understand and Master Their Angry Feelings

In this book we will attempt to map out the times when anger and aggressive feelings surge to the top for children. Most adults think of anger as an ugly emotion, one to keep under cover. Parents are likely to be horrified at their children's displays of hostility and loss of control. Yet anger is not only unavoidable, but necessary. There are many triggers for a child's predictable outbursts, and these become less upsetting when parents can anticipate them and understand how they can help their child learn to get them under control.

Anger not only alerts a child to danger and provides the necessary energy to respond to it, but it is a clear form of expression of himself as a person. Anger, at certain times in his development, becomes a child's way of establishing his independence. Parents will need to understand this purpose and work with it while providing firm limits, so their child can grow up feeling strong and independent, but safe in his outbursts. This book will lead parents through the "touchpoints" of anger—when they surface, and what we need to do about them. At the point where we can't tolerate a child's aggression, our own anger can prompt us to say, "Now it's time for discipline, to make your anger safe." As they help their child understand and master his emotions, parents will use their own as their guide, and as a model for the child.

Learning to handle angry feelings, to channel aggressive urges into constructive action is a lifelong challenge. Parents may be surprised by how early their baby communicates his feelings, how early he senses and responds to theirs. Their job will be to welcome and accept a wide range of feelings, to help the child express them effectively, and to learn that he can handle them safely—on his own.*

The First Angry Feelings

A baby's first angry outburst can come as shock to new parents. This is bound to happen before he's even 4 months old! Remember the first time your baby cried out angrily when you took too long to fetch his bottle? You were taken aback by his

---

*Throughout this book, we will refer to the child as "he" in one chapter and "she" in the next.

sharp new cries and down-turned mouth. In the first months, parents watch for their baby's needy cries—of hunger, pain, boredom, and fatigue—and are ready to respond. But seeing their baby get mad can be a shock. No longer so cute, nor so sweet and innocent, an angry baby is signaling a new way in which he is becoming a person.

The emergence of angry feelings and the aggressive behavior that they sometimes lead to is hardly as eagerly awaited as a baby's first word, or first step. But like those two critically important events, angry feelings and figuring out what to do about them are important ways for him to assert himself and make a place for himself in his world. His parents will have to make room for this new part of his personality. If they can face these feelings, they can also help their baby learn to face them.

Where Do Angry Feelings Come From?

Anger most often arises when our survival or well being appears to be threatened. We seem to have been designed to react this way so that we will recognize our predicament and do something about it. In fact, anger can set off physical responses—flushing, sweating, pounding heart, breathing hard and fast—that push us toward aggressive action.

Sometimes, though, anger leads to action too quickly, without time to think. Aggression can then cause harm that might have been avoided, and may even fail to provide the self-protection that had been its goal. Often we misunderstand and overreact. Or, when feeling entitled, we become irate about something we'd do better to accept. One 4-year-old, disappointed that his birthday party was winding down, stomped into the living room as the last guest left, and to his parents' amazement, mightily toppled over two heavy armchairs. He couldn't accept that his special day wouldn't last forever.

We can all remember such feelings. But limits can help young children learn when they've pushed too far: Discipline becomes the second most important gift parents can give a child. Love comes first, but learning how to rein in strong feelings like anger and disappointment and to live within limits comes next. Birthday presents pale in comparison.

Angry feelings are an internal signal that warns of a threat, real or imagined, from without or within. (The 4-year-old was threatened not only by the end of his party, but also by the overload of excitement within him.) However, when these feelings linger, outlasting their purpose, there is a cost: Later on, a child may become cross, transferring his initial feelings to an unrelated situation, or he may turn inward, and become depressed. Neither of these reactions is readily understood by the child or his parents.

Self-Assertion

Though "aggression" often refers to fighting or other hurtful physical acts, it can also mean simply asserting one's self. It is possible to protect one's self, get what one needs, and realize one's potential, all without hurting anyone. We value a child who is passionate about life and about others, a child who explores, tries out his impulses, and follows his dreams. But as he learns to assert himself in these ways, he needs his parents (or caregivers) nearby to set safe limits on this exploration. He will need to test them. A parent's limits reassure him that he will not be allowed to go too far. Discipline will show him that he will still be cared for in spite of his attempts to separate and become his own person. The tantrums of the second and third years are part of this passionate approach to life. Parents who remember this can see these years as the "terrific twos" instead of the "terrible twos."

Identifying and
Naming Angry Feelings

Children experience irritation, annoyance, frustration, and anger, along with the physical sensations that may go with them, before they have words for such feelings. Even when they do, young children are for the most part too caught up in their busy activity of the moment to be monitoring their own feelings. As a result, they more often seem to be taken by surprise by them, and may need our help to stop, gather themselves, and figure out what the feeling is, where it came from, and what to do about it. Some children seem to do this on their own. Most need a parent's help to find words and use them. We often use terms like "boiling over" or "hotheaded" or "overheated" to convey what it feels like when anger is about to spill into action. Though this may seem abstract, four- and five-year-olds readily understand these images of angry feelings heating up inside. The longer anger lingers without being addressed, the more likely it is to boil over. That's one reason why learning to identify and name feelings early in life are critical skills.

Handling Angry Feelings

When a child knows that he is feeling angry, he has the chance to let others know. But if these feelings overwhelm him, he'll lose control. Then his wailing and flailing will be his way of telling the world how he feels. With his cries, even a newborn can let his parents know when something is wrong, and that they must do something about it. As distressing as this can be for parents, there can also be a sense of relief in knowing that their baby can already alert them to his needs. Some babies can do so more clearly than others. Older children, too, differ in their capacity to register protest in clear, understandable ways that parents will want to respond to.

As they grow older, most children will learn to control themselves long enough to find words to communicate their angry feelings clearly. Sometimes, simply being understood seems to be enough to settle those feelings. At other times, though, the cause of the child's anger needs to be dealt with. "She bit me" or "He took my toy" or "They won't let me play with them" are familiar cries for adult help. Now you can step in and help him learn to handle his anger and resolve the conflict that set it off.

Parents feel the weight of their responsibility to help their child find constructive ways to handle anger. But later he will need to feel confident that he can control his anger on his own. So from the first, think of this as your child's job, though he will need your help. First, he'll need to learn to calm the intensity and physical distress that go with angry feelings, so that he'll be ready for the next tasks: understanding the source of the angry feelings, and figuring out what, if anything, can be done to address the cause.

Temperament and Individual Differences

Each child will have his own unique threshold for reacting to threats of danger, frustration, or humiliation. One child may barely notice a threat, but another may respond by flying into action. A quiet child's response might be to shut down, or to run for cover; an active child might start waving his fists in the air. One child may seem untouched by one slight after another, only to explode later at a far more trivial one, while another may react every time. The speed and intensity of a child's reaction is unique to him, a feature of his temperament. So is the way he settles down and responds to his parents' efforts to calm him.

A child's individual temperament can be understood and taken into account as parents consider how they will help him learn to calm himself, to identify, name, and express his feelings, and to think through a solution to the problem that has set them off. Parents of quiet, accepting children may wish for a more aggressive child, just as parents of an easily inflamed child may wish for a less impulsive one. But for the child, having a parent who accepts and understands his temperament is essential if he is to accept himself.

Ghosts from the Nursery

To help a child recognize his feelings and learn to handle them, parents will need to be open to all of his feelings, and to face their own self-control. For a child's feelings and behavior will, of course, set off our own. We are bound to react, and at times to model less self-control than we would like. This may just be because the child has shocked or offended us. The hurt may run deeper, though, when a child's feelings, or the way he acts on them, call up the "ghosts" from our own pasts.

For example, parents who were bullied as children may sometimes find themselves responding as if they were reliving a childhood memory and being bullied all over again by their small child. Or, a mother of a boy who has been violently mistreated by his father may find that she sees the father's anger in the child. She may feel too frightened to help the boy learn to master his aggressive feelings, or even to believe that this is possible. Parents may also worry that a child's aggression is a sign that he'll follow in the footsteps of a violent adult relative. This, of course, can lead parents to overreact, frightening the child, and making him feel more hopeless about getting his anger under control.

From Culture to Culture:
Expressing Angry Feelings

Expectations for handling emotions such as anger vary from one family to another, from one culture to another. These differences are adapted to the conditions a community faces, and will shape a child's emotional responses. Some cultures, for example, have had to live with constant threats, and as a result their members may always be on guard, or prone to strong reactions. In some cultures, emotions may be expressed intensely, and in rapid succession; in others, they may be held back, or revealed only with great restraint.

Children learn most from the behavior of the adults they admire. Next, they learn from trial and error. Children in most cultures are given chances to make mistakes and to learn from them. Their ability to handle strong feelings will depend, in part, upon whether their families believe they can do so.

Touchpoints of Learning to
Handle Angry Feelings

"Touchpoints" are the predictable stages in a child's development in which rapid spurts of learning occur. Just before each spurt in learning the child is likely to regress to earlier behavior—as the "cost" for the new step he is about take. He and his parents will feel desperate, and they may even fall apart. He's bound to feel undone by this backwards slide, a temporary loss of a previous accomplishment. But these regressions, or "touchpoints," are important opportunities for learning.

A child's ability to control himself is often thrown off track by his efforts to master a new step in another area of development. When a child's angry feelings lead to a temper tantrum or an assault on someone he loves, he frightens himself, and feels ashamed. How terrifying to be at the mercy of such strong feelings, and how embarrassing to be made powerless by them!

His parents will be at a loss to explain why things that had been going so well now seem to be going so wrong. "Will he ever get himself under control?" parents of a young child are bound to wonder. Beneath this question are lurking fears that the inevitable outbursts of these early years will snowball into more dangerous out-of-control behavior in adolescence and adulthood.

The development of self-control over anger and aggressive feelings is not a simple learning process. In Chapter 2, we will trace this process from birth through the years of early childhood. The steps a child takes toward mastering his feelings will be a source of pride, critical to his self-esteem and his sense of independence. Though the process of learning self-control is long and arduous, these early steps are building blocks for the lifelong challenge of handling aggressive feelings. At each step, parents may feel torn between letting the child find his own way and rushing to the rescue. Understanding the child's strengths and vulnerabilities at these moments will help parents make their decisions.

Challenges to Self-Control

As a child grows, he'll discover his potential for aggression. As he learns that he can bite, kick, scream, and throw himself on the ground in a heap, he's bound to try these out. In the process, he'll also learn how each one affects others around him. He'll be especially attentive to how his parents react. Without realizing it, they may reinforce the behavior that bothers them the most. In Chapter 3, we explain common problems such as biting, hitting, kicking, scratching, and temper tantrums as predictable developmental events; we also offer practical suggestions for how to handle them and help a child learn from them. We also describe some of the warning signs of more serious trouble that warrants professional attention. The effects on children of witnessing violence as well as exposure to violence on television and in video and computer games are also addressed in this chapter, along with concrete steps that parents can take to prepare their children for these experiences.

The job of helping children learn how to handle angry feelings and aggression is more critical now than ever before. Adults around the world are failing to control their anger, to listen to each other, to balance their own needs with those of others, and to commit to peaceful resolution of conflicts. Out-of-control anger, violence, hurt, and more anger have paralyzed our world in a deadly cycle of fear and terror. Must we resign ourselves to toughening up our children to survive in a world full of hatred? Can't we prepare them for a different one, a word they'll help make? As parents, we must teach our children to handle their anger, to use their understanding of right and wrong rather than fear, or a thirst for revenge, to guide their actions. We must help them learn to care about those who are more vulnerable than they are, rather than to misuse their own strength.

In recent years, unbridled rage and aggression have hit even closer to home. We have witnessed schoolyard violence wrought by gun-toting teenagers and preteens. As a result, many schools have set up metal detectors to welcome children as they enter. What are we saying to them with these symbols? If they feel that we don't trust them, how can they strive to master their feelings and take responsibility for their behavior?

Self-esteem depends on a child's inner awareness of being able to control his angry, aggressive feelings. As parents, we all want to give our children this sure sense of inner security. Knowing how to get angry feelings under control with pride should be a goal for our children, for all of us. To accomplish this, a parent's job must go far beyond simply stopping or punishing the child. The child must eventually come to understand that he can handle these strong feelings by himself. The "touchpoints" in early childhood when a child learns the steps toward self-control are parents' opportunities to help the child become the master of his anger and aggression.

CHAPTER 2

The Touchpoints of Aggression

During pregnancy, the farthest thought from most expectant parents' minds is that their unborn baby will someday have aggressive feelings and will have to struggle to master them. It will come as a shock later on when they discover that the baby who once seemed so fragile will need help balancing her need for self-assertion with self-control. Yet even during pregnancy, a mother-to-be notices the unborn baby's movements in her womb. "She seems to have a mind of her own," a pregnant woman might say to her husband, her hand probing her belly. A mother-to-be carrying a very active fetus might observe, "Every time I'm ready to lie down and get some rest, she starts zipping around inside me. She won't let me get a wink of sleep and she's not even born yet!"

Even before a baby is born, parents are trying hard to get to know her or him. Every movement is taken as a sign of what the future child will be like. As the fetus moves about in the womb despite the mother's fatigue, is all this kicking and swimming around the earliest instance of self-assertion? No, not as far as anyone can know.

Is a Fetus Already Learning?

A fetus can squirm, but the womb is too cramped for boundless activity. Just as the placenta controls which nutrients the fetus can take in, the motions it can "try out" and "practice" are limited by the uterine walls. As a result, the unborn child's movements become forced into predictable patterns. They start out with simple jerks at first, but over time they become more and more directed. Eventually, the movements evolve into predictable reflex patterns.

These reflexes may even become organized into a sequence—as a response to the bright lights and loud sounds that make their way into the womb during the last part of pregnancy. A fetus reacts, by a startle, or a squirm, or a large stretch, to sounds and lights that reach the uterus. It can also stop responding and shut out unwanted stimulation, or turn toward a more pleasing stimulus. It is tempting to speculate that these responses are being "practiced" and readied for use after birth.

What does this have to do with learning about aggression? Perhaps not much. But it is intriguing to imagine that a fetus might already be learning to channel its responses—to bright lights and loud sounds—to contain them, and to shut them off when necessary. Turning away from such stimulation, or thumb sucking, may be the unborn baby's first opportunity to respond to its environment. Is it too much of a stretch to see the baby's active role in birth as the first act of self-assertion?

The Newborn Touchpoint

The Earliest Feelings: No longer contained by the womb, no longer fed through the placenta, the new baby must learn to express her needs and to enlist the environment to help her survive. The earliest feelings—hunger, cold, discomfort, fatigue, pain— will lead her into action to get what she needs. She finds that if she cries, she can get her hunger satisfied. When she looks into your eyes, reaches out to you, softens and molds into you when you cuddle her, she makes you fall hopelessly in love and ready to nurture her. When she whimpers, startles, and makes angry, dissatisfied faces, someone will wrap her or hold her to calm her down. Will these earliest experiences help her learn to handle such feelings later on?

The Earliest Controls: The newborn already has some control over her sleep and awake states, and the fussy and drowsy states in between. Not long after birth, she can stay alert and pay attention for short periods. She'll look at the walls of her bassinet or gaze into your eyes. But watch a newborn wake up and start to cry. She may finger her satin-bordered blanket, or suck on her fist. These are some of her earliest ways of controlling herself, soothing herself briefly until the stimulation around her overwhelms her efforts. Already, she'll be learning from the comforting you offer, which, in turn, also helps her stay in control—your soft, high-pitched voice, your gentle cuddling, swaddling her when her jerks and startles throw her into distress, nursing her when she cries out in hunger.

When the newborn has absorbed as much as she can of the new sights and sounds around her, she may fall apart. She'll sob, turn red, and sometimes even seem to gasp for breath. Then she may go to sleep. But she may even go to sleep before she starts crying. This is her first way of escaping all the commotion when she needs to. Then she can stay asleep, even if there is more noise and activity around her. She is equipped with the capacity to shut out incoming stimuli through a process called "habituation" (shutting down responses over time to intrusive stimuli).

Learning to Control Awake and Sleep States: The newborn is learning how rewarding it is to get what she needs—milk by crying, sleep by shutting down, cuddling and containment by being active and out of control. Just as important, she is learning how to manage her six awake and sleep states (deep sleep, light sleep, drowsy, alert, fussy, crying). She is learning to stay asleep when she really needs to rest and release tension. She is learning to stay awake so that she can interact with her new world when she wants to learn about it or help caregivers learn about her. Those are the first signs of self-control.

A baby cycles from deep sleep through light sleep, then into fussing, and then alertness for a period. One can watch a newborn baby working to control her motor activity when she suppresses disturbing startles so that she can pay attention to her parents' voices or faces. After she has interacted with an observer, she will try to put her hand up to her mouth to suck on it and maintain a quiet alert state. Her effort to control her state is thrilling to new parents.

After a period of alertness, taking in her world, or reacting with rapt attention in this rewarding state, she will begin to fall apart. She may seem to parents to cry angrily, demandingly. What should you do? Try quieting her with your insistent voice, or by holding her arms. Or try swaddling her so that she can't startle and become frantic with her out-of-control jerking. Maybe she'll need to be picked up, rocked gently, contained in a parent's arms, and even offered a clean finger to suck on. Maybe she'll need to be fed. Maybe it's time for her to be put to bed. Parenting is a process of trial and error. After your efforts, over and over, to find the response that works, the baby will gradually develop the expectation that when she acts, she will receive an appropriate response. She'll know she can count on your help to get back in control.

Earliest Expressions of Needs: A new baby is equipped with six different cries—hunger, discomfort, boredom, fatigue, fussing at the end of the day, and the demanding, piercing cry of pain. Research has demonstrated that new parents can distinguish these six cries after three weeks with the baby. They know that each cry deserves a different response. If her hunger is met by feeding, for example, or boredom by being held in a comforting set of arms, the newborn can then prolong her quiet, alert state. She learns that her own expression of her needs, and her parents' responses, lead to this rewarding state. Over time, the child will learn to meet many of these needs herself by modeling on her parents' early responses. But she will always turn to them, and later to others, to satisfy her need for connection, which will become increasingly evident as she approaches eight weeks.

In the first weeks after birth, parents are already beginning to understand their newborn as a person, as a unique individual. They already recognize that when she looks away, or arches and stiffens, she may be protesting, and is "asking" to be handled differently. She is discovering that she will be taken care of. Though parents may be taken aback when the baby seems angry or upset, they will attend to her. She is not alone. Her parents are learning, too.

3 Weeks

By three weeks, the cycles of sleep and waking are becoming predictable, alternating every three to four hours. But the baby will soon develop a new wrinkle.

End-of-the-Day Fussing ("Colic"):   At the end of a long, demanding day, a 3-week-old grows jerky, oversensitive to noises, to touch, to faces. She'll start to fuss and cry, even for as long as three hours. None of the old maneuvers to stop her crying works for very long. Feeding her more often—as often as every hour or so—works briefly. Then nothing works: She whimpers, she cries, she builds up to a peak of purple-faced crying. Parents feel as out of control as she is.

At first, parents will worry that something is wrong. But pediatricians expect such fussing when a baby is this age. (See *Calming Your Fussy Baby: The Brazelton Way.*) Parents have just started to get to know their baby. Now she seems unreadable, out of control, and angry with them. Her fussing can push parents over the edge. "Why won't she stop crying? Why won't anything work? What can we do?" They feel guilty—of not knowing what to do, of failing to comfort their fragile new baby. Her face screws up as if to say, "Why won't you help me?" After a few hours of this predictable end-of-the-day fussing, the infant quiets down. She eats and sleeps better for the next twenty-four hours. Then, it begins again the next evening.

Parents feel driven to try over and over to quiet her down. Because the crying may be the infant's way of discharging the tension of an inexperienced, overloaded nervous system, desperate attempts to stop it may backfire. Perhaps this is an early version of a child's or adult's build up of feelings that can't be held back, that must find an outlet, preferably a safe one. (Later, there will be punching bags. For now, the baby's parents may need one.)

Once parents can get past their desperation, they'll find that a regular, calm approach can be more helpful. First, pick her up to check for other causes of crying—a wet diaper, a fever, a diaper pin jabbing her. Hold her briefly to soothe her. Feed her a little water to bring up a gas bubble that might be the cause of the distress. Then the baby may need to be put down again. The baby may need to fuss for a period (ten to fifteen minutes). Try this routine every ten or fifteen minutes until she has finally settled herself and released the tension of an overloaded nervous system. Then, a feeding and gentle rocking with a song to sleep will reward her achievement. Finally, she has brought herself under control from a crying state to a quiet one!

Parents should know that although this fussing can recur every evening from 3 to 12 weeks of age, by 12 weeks, it will subside. (If it doesn't, tell your pediatrician.) Then, she'll begin to communicate in other ways. At this same time of day, she'll smile and vocalize responsively instead.

8 to 12 Weeks

The end-of-the-day fussing usually peaks at about 8 weeks, then it starts to diminish. Parents are no longer thrown into panic by this predictable fussing because it seems to follow its own course. But it's still draining.

Now a new phenomenon surfaces! The baby begins to cry angrily when she awakens if she isn't attended to right away. By 8 weeks, she has already accumulated enough experience to build up expectations. She expects to see you when she awakens. She is used to being responded to. "Why don't you come?" she may seem to be saying. Is she angry or just disappointed?

Expressing Needs and Feelings—Effectively: As soon as she sees her parents, she stops crying. She smiles and vocalizes. They realize she can turn one kind of mood into another. She can use the sight of them to be satisfied and to settle herself. They melt. She is beginning to learn other responses—in addition to crying. Parents may feel "manipulated," but proud, too. A little baby who "manipulates" is just doing what she can to get what she needs.

The 8-to-12-week-old is establishing new ways of drawing parents in, and a greater range of responses. She has new ways of controlling herself, and now she can control them, too! They love her new repertoire, and it surely works. When the baby's demands sound new, or even slightly varied, parents' responses are more likely to be forthcoming. They'll want to come see what she's up to now! These early abilities to reach out and draw in her parents deepen their relationship. Now she asserts herself not simply for milk or a dry diaper, but to keep them all connected.

4 to 5 Months

A Steady Schedule and Self-Control: The 4-month-old may be settling down to four feedings a day. She is learning that she can postpone crying by looking around to entertain herself briefly. At 4 months, a baby's vision has adjusted so that she can focus beyond a nearby face, breast, or bottle. Now she can take in a larger swath of her surroundings, and she may even lose interest in feeding as she asserts her new interest in what's going on around her.

She has begun to learn to prolong her sleep and alert waking states, to conform her cycles to her parents' schedules. With these new steps, the baby is discovering her own inner resources—her new ability to wait, to shift her focus, to entertain herself by engaging in her world, to use her own actions to respond to and handle her feelings—of hunger, boredom, fatigue, loneliness. She can reach for a toy. She can play by herself. Briefly.

The Capacity to Protest: By now, the infant knows she can call her parents to her—she can recognize her basic needs and communicate them effectively, an early experience of self-assertion. When something is wrong—she's hungry, wet, unhappy, lonely, or bored—the 4-month-old makes her protests increasingly specific. She has learned from her parents' responses to her. One cry, one facial expression or gesture brings them to cuddle her; another, to change her, and so on. These early experiences of expressing needs and being responded to builds the baby's belief in her ability to affect her world, to act and to know there will be results. Already she is discovering: "I matter!"

Ineffective Protests: What happens when a baby protests only weakly, or not at all? Temperamentally, some babies are quiet, still, and tend to withdraw more than they reach out. They may express their needs less clearly, and their parents will work harder to understand them. Parents will need to watch and listen more closely, to follow the baby's rhythms, to match her quiet ways with theirs. As they gently respond to the subtle cues the baby gives, they will be reinforcing them, encouraging the baby to repeat and build on each successful bidding. Parents whose babies protest more vigorously may be worn out and weary, but can feel more confident that they'll understand their babies' needs. Since such differences appear early, parents of babies whose protests are clear and robust—who let parents know just what they need, who brighten up and respond when someone leans over them—can already feel reassured, and proud.

In addition to temperament, there are other reasons why an infant's capacity to protest may be less effective at times. An infant who is ill, for example, may eventually become too exhausted to cry out in distress or pain. Or she may be effective only in expressing the physical distress that goes with the illness, at the expense of other needs.

Though pervasive developmental disorders such as autism or Asperger's syndrome are rarely detected at this age, it is likely that babies who will receive such a diagnosis in a year or two are already hampered in their ability to communicate their needs and register protest effectively. They are likely to be unable to engage with others. They may seem docile or indifferent and rarely cry out for companionship and entertainment. When they do cry, it may be harder to tell what is troubling them.

Unrecognized Protests: What happens when such 4- or 5-month-old cries are ignored? For example, a baby in an orphanage or other setting where adults are too overwhelmed to respond will begin to stop expecting that her protests will be answered. She will not know what it is like to have her coos and smiles responded to with pleasure. Her cries will become less demanding. She will expect less and less, gradually giving up hope of having her needs met. She is losing out on opportunities to learn how she can behave to affect her world and to deepen her relationships with those who care for her.

As her attempts to reach out fail, so does her self-esteem. Instead of the urgent demanding cries that she might have learned—for food, attention, love—she may already behave as if she expected to fail. Her cry will be fragile, weaker, shortened. She gives up quickly. Her eyes are dull and her face is bland, as if she doesn't expect a response. Instead of signaling what she needs, she waits passively for meals and sleep. All these features may be seen in a hospitalized baby, or one who is poorly attended to in any institution.

Can a 4-Month-Old Be Spoiled?

Parents are bound to wonder. It's hard to spoil a baby of this age. You can avoid it if you don't rush in to pick her up and cuddle her and feed her every time she whimpers. Instead, try to understand what she's asking for, and help her work to be clear in her demands: "What are you fussing for? Do you want a toy? Which toy do you want? The red ball or the rattle?"

Help her wait out her impatience, and discover her motivation to do what she can for herself: "Here's the rattle. Can you reach for it?" You are slowing down your response to her request and helping her discover that she can wait, that she will enjoy her excitement even more after this brief moment of her own patient effort. You are helping her to develop inner resources that she can use to master feelings such as boredom and anger.

You can also help her learn to modulate her cries, to shift from raw frustration, for example, to eager anticipation. When she cries out bitterly, ask her gently, with a glint of humor in your voice, "What do you want?" Talk with her, smile and laugh as you try out one idea after another, and watch to see whether she'll soften her tone as she listens and watches you.

The Rewards of Socializing, and the Cost: At 4 or 5 months, a baby is newly aware of the excitement of interacting with others—for its own sake. Her new abilities to vary and refine her cries, coos, facial expressions, and gestures, along with her growing ability to recognize and respond appropriately to her parents' communications, will push her to reach out for them, to keep testing and enjoying these new skills, over and over.

This is a touchpoint, and there will be a price to pay. Her parents may feel that "she never stops fussing for me." They rationalize, "I think she's beginning to teethe. Why does it bother her so much when no one is nearby?" Parents may feel she is learning to "manipulate" them. But she's just learning the excitement of recognizing and handling her feelings. She is exploring all her new ways of expressing these needs and drawing in others to respond. Each time she reaches out, she learns more about her inner controls and her importance to her world.

8 Months

As a baby of this age learns to crawl, she'll head for the forbidden television set, the stove, the toilet seat. Your "No! No!" will be her incentive to add discovery to her new ability to get around. As she asserts herself, she'll want to know what you think about her accomplishments. Not only can she express herself more clearly now but she can also read what you're thinking in your facial expressions. As she starts to crawl off, she glances up at your face to see how she can change your expression with her own behavior. What power!

As your baby explores the expanding world now within her reach, she needs to know that you're there to protect her from her own urges. As thwarted as she may feel, she's almost grateful to hear you say, "You can't do that. I'll just have to catch you until you can stop yourself." She already knows the limit: "No touching the stove, no touching the TV." She screams angrily when she's stopped, but she looks at you to be sure you are listening and are still determined. She needs you to show her that you are—with a stern face and a serious voice. Her face will relax. She will even cuddle into you when you do.

Each of these little episodes helps a baby learn about her power to make you react, the predictability of your reactions, and your readiness to supply the controls she needs to balance the excitement of exploring. She's paid attention to your warnings, even if she didn't heed them. She's learned she can count on you to stop her, a first step in learning to stop herself. She knows she's safe, and she knows you care!

Pointing: At 8 months, a baby can extend an arm and forefinger and point to what she wants. Now she can use this body language to say, "Look at that. I want you to look at that" or even "Get that for me—*now!*" If her mother is on the telephone, she can creep to the light plug and point a finger at it. Her mother will drop the phone and rush to her—like a puppet on a string, and the baby has discovered that she can pull it. How important this must be to a baby who has been so dependent on others to care for her. At 8 months, she has learned sure ways to assert herself—and cause excitement.

Power of the Pincer Grasp: At this age, a baby is also working on her pincer grasp, picking up tiny bits of food between her thumb and forefinger. So now, of course, she'll practice these new powers to examine, play with, and throw food. She drops bits of finger-food over the side of the highchair. Soon she discovers that she can get her parents to pick it up, or to shout, "Stop it!" Rousing parents to action becomes part of the fun. She's intrigued to discover that they shout louder when she's about to upturn a gloppy custard onto the floor than when she's heaving a Cheerio. She's discovering new powers—over her food, and over her parents! She'll discover that she can even get a dog or a sibling involved too.

There are other new powers to try out. Throwing toys makes a loud crash and a big mess. She can pound on her table to attract attention. She can fuss loudly and kick and twist when she's being diapered. The fun grows when parents get exasperated. "What is going on?" they're bound to wonder. "She used to be such an angel, and now . . . "

What *is* going on? At 8 months, a baby who is learning to crawl, to pick up tiny things, to throw big ones, to make a lot of noise, and to point to what she wants is also now able to recognize the effect she has on her parents with each new exploit. A sense of mastery over her world is on its way. Is she also beginning to test and learn its limits?

These early forms of self-assertion are a big adjustment for her parents. The baby is bound to push herself too far before she learns to hold back. Yet they must handle their exasperation while providing the limits she needs as she tries out her urge for independence with these new abilities. Parents and child are each learning to balance her independence with the boundaries parents must provide. Self-control will have to come later.

12 Months

At 12 months, a baby may have started walking, or is preparing to. This means greater independence and opportunities for daring new exploration. All this can be so exciting that she loses control of herself. She is finding it hard to keep up with the thrill of making her own decisions ("Should I walk over here or over there?"), testing out new ideas ("How about seeing what's inside this closet?"). All these new possibilities are overwhelming. She tries to contain herself, but only feels more frenzied. She knows that she can't control herself without her parents' help, and she'll make sure they know, too. She'll try all sorts of new ways to get her parents as worked up as she is.

Walking around can stir up so much turmoil. She walks, walks, walks, leading her parents around by the nose. When they pick her up or confine her, she screams out in frustration. She may even throw a tantrum, but they will still have to keep her from walking off to potentially dangerous destinations. She'll have plenty of chances to work on controlling her anger, but of course she won't often succeed yet.

A New Kind of Communication—Biting and Hair Pulling: As a baby begins to explore new ways of acting on the world, of expressing herself and finding out what will happen as a result, she is likely to bite her mother. Her mother cries out. The baby is both excited and frightened. "What have I done?" If she's still nursing, she may even bite her mother's breast. A mother may be so startled that she almost drops the baby. "No! No! No!" This reaction can drive the baby to try biting again—and again. Gradually she may learn how to stop biting, but only if the parent reacts firmly. "No! That hurts" and puts the baby down. Walking away is a powerful punishment.

Hair pulling may also start at this age. It brings an immediate response. "Ouch!" any parent will shriek. The baby giggles. She'll do it again. They'll cry out, "No! No!" She grins but she may stop. "Will they stick by me even if I try it again?" she may seem to wonder. She is discovering the mixed pleasure of creating a commotion and annoying her parents. She is also testing new ways of communicating with parents as her new readiness for separation complicates her connection to them.

Aggression and the Touchpoint of Learning to Walk: At about a year, as she focuses her energy on the big developmental step of learning to walk, sleeping, feeding, and early emotional controls all may be disrupted. Suddenly, she'll refuse to go to sleep and start waking up in the middle of the night. She wakes to call out as she pulls up on her crib rails every four hours. "Help me! I want to practice my walking!" she seems to say. She loses interest in food. Instead of whimpering, she screams for help. She falls apart easily.

Learning to walk exacts a price from everyone in the family. For parents, sleep is wrecked. Parents will be angry with the child. "Why has she suddenly become so demanding?" "Whatever happened to our easygoing baby?" The child is on the verge of walking, but can't quite yet. Her desperate frustration turns into angry and insensitive demands that she makes on everyone around her.

If parents can see these changes as temporary, and as evidence of the passion that she is putting into learning to walk,

Learning to Walk: Ways Parents Can Help

1. Walking is an early form of self-assertion. "I want to go where *I* want to go, when *I* want to go there," the 12-month-old seems to say. So she's bound to resist your efforts to make her go somewhere when *you* need her to. She's more likely to go along with you, though, if you prepare her for transitions. At this age, she'll need only a few minutes' warning. Let her know that you understand she doesn't want to stop what she's doing, even though soon she'll have to. Let her bring a favorite toy with her to the next activity if you can, and tell her about what you'll be doing next to help her switch gears.

2. Comfort her when she's not demanding. This way it will be easier to hold off on comforting when she whines and fusses for it. At those times you'll want to intervene less, so that she can learn to soothe herself, and so that you don't reinforce this behavior. However, during this touchpoint, your child will at times fall apart and be unable to comfort herself. Then you'll need to go to her. Take her in your arms quietly. Do as little as you can to see what she can do on her own to settle down. When she's calm, let her know she can ask for hugs when she needs them without making a fuss.

3. Allow the baby to practice her new skill day and night. There's no stopping a baby who is about to walk. She'll pull herself up on the couch, the coffee table, the bathtub during the day, the crib rail at night, anything within reach, whether it can support her weight or not. Watch out!

continues on next page

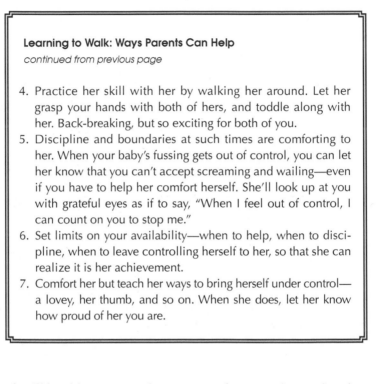

Learning to Walk: Ways Parents Can Help
continued from previous page

4. Practice her skill with her by walking her around. Let her grasp your hands with both of hers, and toddle along with her. Back-breaking, but so exciting for both of you.

5. Discipline and boundaries at such times are comforting to her. When your baby's fussing gets out of control, you can let her know that you can't accept screaming and wailing—even if you have to help her comfort herself. She'll look up at you with grateful eyes as if to say, "When I feel out of control, I can count on you to stop me."

6. Set limits on your availability—when to help, when to discipline, when to leave controlling herself to her, so that she can realize it is her achievement.

7. Comfort her but teach her ways to bring herself under control—a lovey, her thumb, and so on. When she does, let her know how proud of her you are.

they'll be able to survive her angry outbursts and even their loss of sleep without feeling so desperate and hurt. If they can understand the reason for the baby's fragility and angry behavior, they can find their role in helping her through this "touch-point," through this period of reorganization.

As a child negotiates a touchpoint, aggressive feelings may come to the surface. Such feelings can be part of the price the child must pay for the exciting new step she is about to take. In the midst of this touchpoint, a baby may scream or collapse when you walk away from her. She is more sensitive to the times you must leave her because now she knows she can leave you.

Walking and Object Permanence: With this new conquest, a baby can try to test out a new concept. "If I leave her, will she still be there?" She's discovering *object permanence*—that an object or a person still exists when it's hidden from view. She needs to test this out. Even though parents are around the corner, she needs to be sure that they're still there. Can she count on them to be within calling distance when she can't see them? Now a child of this age may start "disappearing." Is she trying to provoke her parents and to see whether they'll come to find her? She needs to test her parents now more than ever. She hungers for the reassurance of their limits now that she has discovered she can get away.

Separations: Walking, the power to "disappear," and the discovery that she can think about people and things even when they are not there change the meaning of separation for the toddler.

Leaving a child at the childcare center has been relatively easy until now. Parents could hand her over into the arms of a familiar caregiver. She saved her protest about being left until the end of the day when her parents returned. Out of sight, out of mind.

But at a year, a child is likely to begin to fight to keep her parents near. She has learned she can leave her parents, making them "disappear" as she toddles around a corner. Gone—for the briefest moment. But she can still think of them, still keep them in her mind. Now she must also face what will happen when they leave her. This is a fearful new concept. The child knows now that her parents will be somewhere, but not with her, all day long. She knows that she will miss them, cry out for them, but be unable to make them come back until they decide it's time.

A baby of this age is no longer content to let her parents know at the end of the day how she feels about being left. Now she asserts herself before they leave to see whether she can hold on to them. First, she tries out a whimper on the way into the center. She feels her mother stiffen, or her father become stern. Her protest escalates. Soon it's a full-blown tantrum over being left—even with someone she knows and cares about. She has learned by now that it's a sure way to make a parent linger before she is left. A small reward for having to say goodbye and wait all day for her parents' return.

A 1-year-old baby has now learned that her protests are heard, even if they are not responded to as she would like. Protest and testing out her parents' feelings and actions—they'll miss her, too, and will return, but now they must go—help her handle her angry feelings about being left. Protest also expresses her connection to her parents.

Limits: Discipline is a critical part of being cared for. Protests against separations, and the separations themselves, are made safer by parents' limits. Although a child's demands have been heard, and are understood, a limit is set: Parents must go, though they will return. As a result, the child will come to realize that these separations will not hurt her or her parents. She will be okay, and so will they, and she can count on their daily reunions. But if parents give in to a child's demands not to leave, the message is confusing. The child may wonder whether her fear was well founded, if something bad would happen if her parents did leave. Is separating dangerous? Is that why they decided to stay? Now, she might worry, if they do leave, maybe they really will never return.

From a year of age on, a child will experience more and more feelings that must not be satisfied, no matter how clearly she expresses them. Parents will find it increasingly trying—and increasingly necessary—to hear the child out, and then to help her accept it when she can't always have her own way.

16 to 18 Months

This is the age of "Me. Me try. I wanna do it. Lemme do it." The toddler's acts of self-assertion have a new and daring edge! Now, when she bites her mother or hits her father, her gestures seem far less accidental, tentative, or exploratory. Instead, she seems to be taking a stand, as if to say, "What are you going to do about it?" By now, parents are bound to react firmly.

A child of this age has one idea after another and needs to try them out right away. As she tries out her new walking, she'll want to stomp off on her own. She's off like a rocket toward the street! If she's been near streets before, she should already know better; if she doesn't, she'll find out now that her parents will stop her angrily and firmly: "Never do that again!" And maybe she won't. But parents should not count on her curbing herself. Not yet.

In the second year, the child works hard to learn so much—about herself as a separate individual, about her need for her parents, and how to become independent without losing them. By provoking her parents and pushing them away, she tests whether they will still be there for her.

She'll have to count on her parents to understand what she cannot about her own needs. Her drive to try things out for herself, to see how far she can go, depends on being able to fall back on her parents. This is an intense time for the child, and a tense one for parents. Underlying the child's intensity is her struggle to feel in control of her wishes and her impulses. With this comes the excitement of "I can make my own decisions!" but also a new vulnerability. It's exhilarating but frightening. Parents are torn between encouraging her independent forays and supplying the safety net of discipline, limits, and affection that the child needs.

Why are the child's feelings stronger than ever now? It's not just that she's torn between wanting to try things out on her own and needing to be cared for; she is also more able to focus on what she wants, and to stay focused on it with increasing persistence. Gone are the days when she could easily be distracted from what she couldn't have to something she could. This is another touchpoint. The new ability to focus and persist, and to resist distractions, allows her to pursue her interests with more determination. But she and her family will pay a price in the form of the outbursts that erupt—with each change, with each transition to a new activity, each time she must stop.

In the second year, the child's feelings are more powerful than ever. She is not yet ready to identify them, express them effectively, and often can't hold back on acting on them. Tantrums are the result. Parents can turn these into early opportunities for learning to handle strong feelings, put up with frustration, and develop self-control.

Tantrums: (See also *Tantrums and Self-Control* in Chapter 3.) When a child first throws herself down and into a tantrum, she'll finish it with a look of helpless vulnerability. When the episode is over, she needs the sturdy, calm protection of loving arms immediately afterward. "Falling out," as tantrums are sometimes aptly called, takes a lot out of the child. She becomes pale, limp. She clings. She whimpers as her mother picks her up to cuddle her. In the midst of a tantrum, though, this won't help.

The child is frightened by her own loss of control. Maybe this is why she may try tantrums again and again—until she learns to control herself. She is seeking mastery over the power of her own feelings and the frightening behavior they unleash. Each time she has a tantrum, she gets a reaction. She learns from this when and where her parents are least able to help her calm down and pull herself together. These times and places are the most overwhelming and the most frightening for the child. Inevitably, tantrums erupt where they will make the most impact—at the grocery store, in a moving car, in a crowded bus or subway, or at a boisterous birthday party: all the most inconvenient, mortifying times and places for parents.

Tantrums are more likely to occur when a child is tired, hungry, stressed, and over-stimulated—and when parents are, too. Then, if she's frustrated, if she can't get her way or what she wants, a tantrum is likely to occur.

Tantrums may be caused by internal struggles. In the second year, a child who so badly wants to do things "all by myself," to make her own decisions, will be overwhelmed when faced with her own inability to make up her mind: "Will I or won't I?" "Do I or don't I?" Tantrums arising from such intense ambivalence can come from within without warning. A child may stand in the middle of a doorway and look into one room, then the other. She can't decide: "This way or that way?" All of a sudden, she falls down to cry out and thrash. She looks tortured. Tantrums like these surprise everyone around the child. She was the only one who cared what she did next. No one else even noticed. If a parent tries to comfort her, she prolongs her tortured screaming and flailing. It's as if she were saying, "Leave me alone! This is *my* decision!"

Parents are bound to question themselves: "What in the world have I done? How can I prevent these blow ups?" It helps to see that the struggle comes from within the child. Having her own way—even if she's not sure what that would be—is her new approach to asserting her independence. It's coupled with a newfound rebellion against feeling helpless. But the harder the child fights against her parents, and against feeling helpless, the more helpless she becomes; and so she throws herself on the floor and dissolves into tears. A tantrum can seem like a desperate attempt to fight off such feelings, but it's a losing battle.

Biting and Hitting: (See *Biting* and *Hitting, Kicking, and Scratching* in Chapter 3.) Biting and hitting may become bigger problems now. When a child of this age builds up to a peak of excitement or frustration and loses control of herself, she is likely to lash out and scream or hit or bite. When, after losing control, she attacks another child on a play date, she is as surprised as the child she's attacked. When her playmate dissolves into tears, she is as frightened as the other child. She has never had such a response from adults. She didn't mean to hurt. She just had to let off steam. But it's frightening.

Everyone looks at her as a pariah now. Other parents may react: "She bites. I don't want her to play with my child." "I don't want my child to learn about hitting from her. What a bad example for my child!" Yet most toddlers go through such a phase. Do they "learn" it from each other? Maybe, but it is so common that it seems more likely that it is a nearly universal impulse.

How can parents help a child regain control and learn not to hit or bite? Parents' or caregivers' reactions add to the child's anxiety when they become as excited as the child. Where can she turn? She needs a caring adult's comfort, limits, and reassurance that she can learn to control herself.

This is a time for discipline, for teaching. If you can recognize the early warning signs that lead to hitting or biting, you can pick your child up and help her calm down *before* she lashes out at another child. If you can comfort her beforehand, you can help her learn to control this behavior, to hold back on these impulses. Eventually, she'll even learn to recognize her own warning signs and to pull back before it's too late.

When it's too late to stop her, you can still teach her that trying to hurt someone is not acceptable. After such an episode, stay calm. Pick up the child to hold and contain her. After she bites or hits, separate the children and let your child know that she'll have to stay by herself until she can apologize and keep herself under control. This kind of brief isolation is more effective than overreactions that can make her loss of control more frightening to her, or lead her to test out these responses with more biting.

When she can hear you, speak to her calmly but firmly: "That hurts. You just can't do that to someone else. When you're calm, you go and tell her you're sorry. Next time, I'll try to help you *before* you lose control." She may be fearful of her inability to stop herself, and this is bound to undermine her efforts to try. You can reassure her that she *can* learn to stop herself, and until then, that she can rely on your limit: "I can't let you do that."

2 to 3 Years

A child this age can seem so serious sometimes. Her frown, her determined pace as she walks, let you know that she's trying hard to figure out her world. She decides what she wants and worries that she may have to struggle to get it. Sticking to her decision matters more than whatever it is she thought she wanted. She tries maneuvering around her parents' commands. But she loves them. They are so caring and tender when she isn't in battle with them. She is torn between her hunger for their affection and her need to assert herself. And often that means she has to show them how serious she is.

When her parents try to quash one of her new ventures—rearranging the furniture, for example, or putting the potato flakes in the soap dispenser, she is ready to rebel. She seeks new ways of maintaining this precious independence.

Toilet Training: Toilet training can be an opportunity for self-assertion: "You don't have to change me. I can go all by myself." The child may be excited about the chance to identify with this world of grownups. But children who have been pushed to be toilet trained may not see this as an opportunity to become more independent. For them, using the potty may seem like another instance of "giving in." They are more likely to resist, or to feel they are being controlled.

Parents may not realize what they are asking of a child when they push her to be toilet trained. Asking a child to feel it coming on, get where we tell her to go, and then watch that part of her body (the stool) disappear for the rest of her life! What a request. It's got to be her decision. Why wouldn't a feisty child resist? Why wouldn't she hold on to her bowel movements? When she does, she's likely to become constipated. When she does go, the hard stools may hurt her, leaving tiny tears in her anus. She'll scream, "No! No! No! It hurts! It hurts!" Then, in addition to her need to assert her will, she'll have another reason not to go.

If they've been pressured before they are ready, children may refuse to use the potty, to withhold their stools, or even to smear them. These signs of resistance are children's passionate pleas to be allowed to assert themselves and master their own toilet training. A child may withhold her bowel movements as if to say, "This is part of *me*. I want to be in charge of it myself." Parents may beg the child, "Just try it! Just sit here for a little bit. Do it for Mommy." They may try to bargain and persuade: "Mommy can't bring you to preschool if you're in a diaper."

If you've had a struggle like this, try apologizing to your child for your pressure. Let her know it's up to her to decide when she's ready. Hold back on your reminders to use the toilet, no matter how gentle. Be sure to consult her physician or nurse practitioner for help in keeping her stools soft so that she won't try withholding bowel movements to avoid pain (see *Toilet Training: The Brazelton Way*, listed in the *Bibliography*).

When you leave toilet training to the child, she can decide on her own timing, and then live up to her own decision. It will be her achievement. You will have helped her turn resistance to your pressure into her own decision making, her own declaration of independence. Toilet training can become an opportunity to let a child feel in charge of her own body.

Tantrums: (See also *Tantrums and Self-Control* in Chapter 3.) Two-year-old "falling out" episodes may begin to seem less like a loss of self-control and more like the child's assertion of her ability to control you. Now she'll have a tantrum to show you how important it is to her to make her own choices: "I want the orange shirt, not the green one." You'll have to pick your battles. When she is crossed or frustrated, she may save up her feelings, only to explode later. It will be harder for both of you to know where it came from.

Don't be surprised, though, if she still melts down when she can't get her way, or any time you say no: "No, you can't go out in your shirt and socks. It's raining." A 3-year-old may still fall down screaming. But the tantrums have a new element now. As she throws herself on the ground, she may seem to do so with a dramatic flair. A tantrum is a communication. The child will look her parents straight in the eye. With a new defiance, she asserts her ability to subject them to a tantrum that only she can control. At times she almost seems to be demanding that this new power be recognized. If parents give in, her tantrum will usually stop, but she'll have more power than she can handle.

Even now, tantrums are no more fun for the child than for her parents. She resorts to them when she doesn't know how else to get her way. A parent's job is to help the child learn other ways of expressing her needs, and to put up with not always getting her way.

It will help to let her make her own decisions and feel in control—but only when you can. For example, let the child press the elevator button, but not all of them. Let her make simple choices when whatever she chooses will be acceptable. "No, we're not buying soda or chips. But you can decide if we should get pears or apples. Both? Okay." Be clear when it's not up to her. Then, when you must step in and decide for her, she can still fall back on these experiences.

Don't take tantrums personally. If you do, you'll be making them more powerful. Instead, stay cool, and, by your lack of response, disarm her. Just let her know: "Your tantrum won't get you what you want." Stick to your position. Then, if it's safe, walk away. If not, stay nearby and keep an eye on her, but don't interact. Your resolve will be a relief to her. Afterward, pick her up and comfort her.

New Expectations: A child of this age has learned so many new ways to show control over her world, but now there are new expectations. For example, pulling the cat's tail, pinching Daddy, or kicking Mommy when she tries to pick her up may once have seemed playful or overlooked. Now, though, the child is expected to understand that these actions are hurtful and that she will be held responsible because everyone thinks she should know better. When she kicks or pulls, it is assumed that she "did it on purpose." Whether she did or not, she now needs these new expectations.

Some Causes of Anger That Lingers

If your child seems unable to enjoy her time with peers, and is angry or irritable most of the time, this may be a sign of trouble that needs your attention:

- Anger may be a signal that the child feels threatened and is seeking protection.
- There may be a simple or obvious cause, such as the arrival of a new baby in the family.
- There may be a cause that is more difficult to face, such as hostility between two parents having trouble with their marriage.
- The child may have a delay in language development that prevents her from expressing her needs and leaves her overwhelmed with frustration.
- Another possibility is that she is frightened—by an older child who teases or bullies her, or by some even more serious threat.

If necessary, consult your pediatrician or a teacher who knows your child for help finding out what's behind her aggression.

Even though she is not always able to control herself, she needs to know that she is responsible for her behavior. This shows respect for her strong wish to be in control, and to be in control of herself.

There may be all kinds of reasons for such aggressive behavior. Here are a few common triggers:

- Getting attention
- Anger over being thwarted in play

- Sensory overload or fatigue at the end of the day
- Self-defense—against a threat, imagined or real

But none of them excuses hitting and pinching.

Expectations must be clear. When a child hits, or pinches, or bites, for example, the consequences must be swift, firm, and consistent. When a child resorts to physical fighting over and over, or seems unable to shift from this mode to a more peaceful one on play dates, parents need to look for underlying reasons. A child's repeated attacks on you or on others may be her only way of telling you that something more serious is bothering her.

4 Years

A 4-year-old knows that she matters. She no longer needs her earlier defiance. She can handle her feelings with less effort now, and can more easily make her needs known. Now that she is less focused on herself, she is curious about the world. She can only understand it, though, in terms of her own experience. But she can look more deeply now, and sustain her interest for longer.

Turning Against One Parent and Toward the Other: A 4-year-old is still terribly busy. Yet she seems more relaxed. Her face is softer and more confident. A boy will swing his arms, stretching out his legs like his daddy. A girl has smoother motions and makes gestures like her mommy's. Perhaps 4-year-olds are absorbed more now with identifying with one parent and then the other than with asserting themselves in defiant rebellion. Instead, 4-year-olds assert themselves by their careful study, first of one parent, then the other. You are bound to feel rejected when she identifies with you and tries to take your place. Try not to show it. Go with the flow. It won't last.

At 4, a child will turn her back on one parent, but be "in love" with the other. This is her way of identifying with the parent she has temporarily rejected. Afterward, she'll turn to the other parent in the same exclusive way. This is her way of learning all about one parent at a time. It's so economical to concentrate on one and ignore the other. If it is pointed out to her, she's liable to say, "You're a bad mommy. My daddy's the only one who loves me." She is beginning to see that she can be hurtful with such talk.

The Dawn of Conscience: More aware of others, the 4-year-old is watchful, almost on guard, as she monitors those around her for their reactions. She may realize that one parent feels jilted when she throws all her passion into getting close to the other one. At 4, a child is developing the ability to imagine the thoughts and feelings of others. She can begin to see, now, her ability to affect them. "If I hit her, she won't want to play with me. If I take her toy, she'll scream and Mommy will blame me." She worries. She wants to have friends. She tries. Parents will swell with pride when they see their child reenact in her play the caring she has received from them. One more reason why they are so upset by the angry explosions still so inescapable at this age.

This is another touchpoint. Now a child can judge the effects of her behavior with a better understanding of its consequences, a new sense of right and wrong. With this awareness comes the dawn of a conscience. Guilty feelings are new, too. They can be a powerful motivator.

A 4-year-old can, at times, hold back on her urges to assert herself, to stomp on others' territory and declare it her own. More often now she is able to control her aggressive impulses and respect the feelings of others. As a result, she feels a new self-confidence.

Emotional Intelligence: A 4-year-old has also begun to be aware of her own feelings and to pay attention to them. She has more words to describe them. As she learns to name her feelings as they well up inside her, she has a chance to think about them, what they are telling her, why she is having them, and what she can do about them. This is the beginning of an important new ability that some psychologists have called "emotional intelligence." It is also critical to learning to handle her aggressive urges.

Learning to Share: A 4-year-old will still need help in learning how to balance her needs with those of others. She'll need help in learning how to handle situations that are bound to produce conflicts. Some of these can be avoided. A parent might say, for example, "If we have your friend over to play this afternoon, you and I have to decide which toys you'll share. Remember how you fought last time so she wouldn't play with your toys? If you don't want her to play with some of your toys, let's put them away before she gets here." She listens to this argument, and she may cooperate. Occasions like this will help her learn to plan. Anticipating solutions to potential conflicts can give her the chance to avoid a predictable crisis.

The Cost of a 4-Year-Old's Aggression: Now that she is beginning to be aware of her aggressive feelings, and of their consequences, the 4-year-old may be frightened of herself. Her aggressive acts carry a new cost! As she tries them out, she is fearful. She knows she's wrong, and she expects to be punished.

At night, when her defenses are down, when she is regressing to a helpless sleep state, fears and nightmares begin to surface. "Is that a witch under my bed? Is there a monster in the closet?" In her nightmares, they may be coming after her to punish her for her "bad" behavior. Or they may be aggressive in all the ways she'd like to be but knows she shouldn't.

I remember a little boy who hit a best friend and knocked her down. The victim got a small but bleeding cut on her arm. Everyone rushed to comfort her, to wash her arm with peroxide, to find brightly colored bandages for her. Her attacker had retreated to a corner of the schoolyard. Sucking his thumb, he was pale, downcast, breathing heavily. When I picked him up to cuddle him, he laid his head on me (a perfect stranger) and sobbed. He felt scared and isolated by the ruckus he'd caused. That night, I later learned, he had a long nightmare—full of wild animals, barking dogs, little boys with broken arms and legs.

Fears that are near the surface—of being "bad" and hurtful, of deserving punishment—will be called up during the day by any frightening event, even a dog barking or an ambulance's siren. Thunder and lightning terrify a child of this age. To her it sounds like an angry scolding from someone who sees and hears all the "bad" things she's done.

At night, fears like these overwhelm her. She is aware of her ability to hurt others. She is frightened of her own fantasies of being more powerful than she really is. At this age, losing control is more frightening than ever. Conscience and being aware of other's feelings have made it seem more dangerous.

How Parents Can Help with Nightmares: A 4-year-old needs to be nurtured and coddled at night, when her defenses are down, when she's more vulnerable. Don't give up routines— reading, cuddling, singing. Respect the fears that reflect all the struggles of the day. Reassure her ahead of time that you'll come when her fears pop up. If she calls out at night, go to her. "I'm here and you don't need to worry." Listen to her fears and her attempts to understand them.

Discipline is reassuring and even more important through this period. When parents are clear and consistent about rules and expectations, the child will know that "someone else is in control" even if she is not!

Helping a Child with Nightmares

1. During the day, look for monsters and witches under the bed and in the closet with your child. This is one way to show that you can take her worries seriously without reinforcing them.
2. At bedtime, read stories that help children understand nightmares, such as *There's a Monster in My Closet.* You can also read stories about dreams—such as *In the Night Kitchen*— because they help children understand that dreams come from the worries and other feelings we store up during the day. There are also other books that remind a child about how delightful dreams can be. (See the *Bibliography.*)
3. Show your child where the nightlight is. Shut off all the other lights and let her look around while you are still there.
4. Reassure her that you'll be in your room while she's in hers.
5. If she does wake up with a nightmare, go to her. Sit by her bed. Let her tell you about it. (My mother used to say that if you tell someone about your nightmare, it won't come back. I think she was right.)

Helping a Child with Fears

1. Don't put off facing a fear. Waiting will only make the child think that there really is something to worry about.
2. Make a list with your child of all the ways she's learned to make herself feel better when she is scared: for example, holding your hand, talking together, trying to think of something different, or of times when facing the fear has helped. These are self-comforting strategies.

continues on next page

Helping a Child with Fears
continued from previous page

3. Then, make a list of all the things that are scary about the feared object or event, and rank them from most scary to the least: for example, "I hate when the dog barks, I hate just seeing the dog—especially when she shows her teeth, I hate seeing her dog bone in the yard when she's not there, I even hate just thinking about her."
4. Now your child is ready to face her fear. She can think first about the least scary aspect of the feared object or event and then practice all her self-comforting strategies. Once she can calm herself while thinking about the least frightening part of the fear, she's ready to move on to the next. Step by step, she'll be able to conquer her fear.

Children Learn from Parents' Modeling: You can tell your child about the times when you were afraid (if they're not too scary) and how you faced your fears. You can also tell her about your own attempts to curb your own aggressive feelings so that she can identify with you and model them. She will learn most about her aggressive feelings from you. During the daytime, let her see you get upset but then get yourself back in control. "I get so angry with our neighbor when he throws his weeds over our fence. I could smash him. But I don't. I just clear them out. I tell him it bothers me. He doesn't like to hear it, but I feel better when I do." Watch her next time she loses control to see how much she's learned from you. Help her notice her new success when she holds back an angry impulse. Can't she feel proud?

Handling Aggression After the Dawn of Conscience: If a child is out of control, or if she really hurts another child, safety and containment come first. Stop the action, which may mean separating the children, and even briefly isolating them. Then limits: "Stop hitting." If she doesn't, you'll immediately need to intervene and physically separate the children. "I meant what I said. Hurting someone else is not okay." When she's ready to hear it, she'll need consequences, too: an apology, and maybe having to play alone until she's ready to play with others without hurting them. But an out-of-control child will also need your understanding. Help the child see how much she has done to try to bring herself under control, even if she has failed, and let her know that she can build on this. "I know you tried. I know how badly you feel. Maybe next time you'll be able to do it."

Repeated aggressive acts such as hitting or biting or scratching may be a signal that a child needs help. Talk to her about this behavior. Let her talk to you. It will help her to know that you want to help, that you will still be there for her—no matter what. (See *Hitting, Kicking, and Scratching* in Chapter 3.)

Aggressive Fantasies—Toy Guns: Parents in my practice were disturbed when a 4-year-old left a toy gun in my office. The

Discipline for Aggressive Behavior

- Contain the child and stop the behavior—decisively, consistently. Separating the children, and isolating them briefly, may be necessary. (Sometimes a child may even need to be held. See *Tantrums and Self-Control* in Chapter 3 for a safe way to do this.)
- Firmly state the rule, even if the child already knows it: "No hitting." Later, make sure she can repeat it, and that she understands why it is so important: "We treat other people the way we want them to treat us" is one approach. "It isn't right to hurt people" is another. But first she'll need to calm down.
- Pay attention to the child's emotional state. Help her to do the same. If she's still worked up, can she recognize this? Does she know what she can do to settle herself? You may need to remind her.
- When she is calm, she'll be ready to learn. Now it's time for discipline. Discipline is teaching. Help her look at what happened, what went wrong. What were the warning signs? How can this be avoided in the future? Can she list some of the warning signs she'll be looking out for? Help her see her own responsibility. Help her believe she can control herself by letting her know that you believe she can.
- Decide on consequences that fit the "crime." An apology is in order, and a heartfelt one is best. The child may need time away from the one she has hurt so that she can think over the other ways of handling conflicts that you have discussed. You might even need to talk through a few predictable scenarios and find out how she thinks she would handle them now: "What if she won't let you play with her toys next time? What will you do then?"

continues on next page

Discipline for Aggressive Behavior
continued from previous page

- Forgiveness: Accepting a child's apology is a way to restore her belief in her own "goodness." She also needs to know that you have hope for her progress. A child who believes that others think she is "bad" will come to believe it herself. Then she is sure to act that way.
- Watch for underlying reasons for hurtful behavior.
- If your child hurts others repeatedly or is cruel to a family pet, doesn't seem remorseful, has trouble making and keeping friends, seems angry and irritable most of the time, or is preoccupied with violence, talk with your pediatrician. Because your child could suffer from depression, or have a developmental delay, or dwell on a haunting traumatic experience, she may need to be referred to a child psychologist or psychiatrist.

boys all gravitated to it. Girls ignored it, preferring the doll house. I was intrigued by the boys' interest, so I kept the gun. Parents asked, "Do you approve of guns?" "No," I'd answer. "Then why do you allow one in your office? Don't you think it gives the message to kids that guns and aggression are okay?"

I explained that I didn't think you could keep 4- and 5-year-olds from playing with toy guns. Even if they don't have a toy gun, children (especially boys) of this age will make them, or pretend they have one. They see guns on television. They are eager to be like the tough guys in the shows. Playing out these fantasies now may be better than waiting until later. Four-year-olds feel so small, and know how easily they can be overpowered. Of course they wish they could be tough.

I'm never surprised when a 4-year-old boy marches into my office, his thumb and forefinger cocked to look like a gun; it's as if he wants to say, "Take it easy, Doc, I'm in control here!" It seems like an important statement—not about guns or violence, but about being scared and needing to feel protected—in the stressful situation of a doctor's office. I don't think we are really encouraging violence when we understand this kind of meaning behind a child's play.

Nonetheless, we can help children this age begin to understand the difference between make-believe and the real world. At this age, though, they can't possibly understand the reality that death is forever. Forever is too long for any of us to comprehend. Four-year-olds are more likely to think that death is like sleep, and that sooner or later, a dead person will wake up. But we can urge them to think over whether they'd really want to hurt someone. And we can help young children learn to value and enjoy richer and more varied play than just shooting each other, or beating each other up, over and over. They can learn to listen to each other, to share, to teach, to comfort, to share their angry feelings openly, and to understand each other as they model these relationships on those they have with their parents. (See *Toy Guns, Action Figures, and Other Aggressive Toys and Games* in Chapter 3.)

5 to 6 Years

Passive Aggression

A 5-year-old feels like a "big girl" until she thinks about it. But when she does, she feels so small. "How can I get bigger quicker?" She wants to grow up so badly. She's bound to try out new ways of feeling older and more powerful than she is—lying, perhaps, or the more subtle ways of getting what she wants that are available to her now, at 5: dawdling, whining, sulking, and pouting.

Why these new ways now? Tantrums are for smaller children—too humiliating for a 5-year-old. Unlike 2- and 3-year-olds, whose goal is to assert their independence, children of this age want to feel "grown-up" by being like their parents. They want to please them. Five-year-olds are aware enough of others now to know how their behavior will affect other people. They are more apt to hold back when they know they're about to do something wrong or displeasing. This leads them to discover more passive, and often more effective forms of aggression. These allow them to try to get their way without asserting themselves or taking responsibility for upsetting others. This is a touchpoint—the child's new awareness, and deft new strategies that lead to turmoil for child and parents alike.

Dawdling: On a school morning, a 5-year-old dawdles, drags her feet to get dressed, brush her teeth, and come downstairs to breakfast. These are her ploys, as her parents rush to ready themselves for work, to delay the inevitable separation of going to school. What can parents do? First of all—don't nag. Your child will end up preferring your negative attention to no attention at all. Instead, make breakfast a shared family time that children enjoy and look forward to. The night before, lay out her clothes with her. In the morning, let her know how much time she has, and give her matter-of-fact reminders: "Five more minutes. One more minute." You could even put a timer in her room to help her keep track without you. When dawdling is a problem, be sure to build in plenty of extra time. Your child has more power over you than she should if you feel panicky about getting everyone ready in time. It may sound drastic, but it can turn out to be a relief to get up fifteen minutes earlier every morning so that breakfast and good-byes are not a tense time for everyone.

Begging and Whining: Begging and whining are effective ways for a child to get what she wants—if her parents give in. Repeated grating pleas can wear parents down, especially when they are tired, stressed, and in a hurry. Grocery shopping can be a risky time. "Why can't I have a candy bar? Please just one. I promise I won't ask you next time. You let me have one last time. I'll brush my teeth when we get home. I'll even use my own money. Please. Just one." Over and over. Such insistence can debilitate a parent. Exasperated, parents will lose their tempers. Or they may begin to think of reasons to justify giving in. "She's tired. Shopping is boring. Why not give in, just this once?"

Don't. You'll regret it. You'll be teaching your child that whining and begging are acceptable and effective means to her ends. Limits are critical. You are the parent. You can either ignore her whining completely or leave the store. Or you can tell her, calmly but sternly, "You are whining. You will not get what you want by whining. Ever." Then, stick to it.

Next time, set a limit before you go. "Remember how you beg for candy when we go to the grocery store? We don't buy candy at the grocery store. We buy food. No matter how much you whine. If you ever do want me to get you something you want, whining and begging won't work. You can ask for something once, and then that's it. Even when I say no." Be sure you live up to this. You're protecting the child from her own disappointment! (The best policy is never to pick up candy at the checkout counter. Every time you do, your child will have hope for the next time, and will be more disappointed when you don't. The result—more whining. Ugh!)

Sulking and Pouting: When a 5-year-old refuses to respond to a request and mopes around, sulking and pouting, parents are stymied. Such quietness can make a child seem so vulnerable to parents. Children sense their parents' concern. An aggressive child who resorts to sulking can startle her parents. "What is wrong?" they'll wonder. It's a powerful maneuver.

When a parent ignores sulking and pouting, they lose their value to the child. If the child continues to glare in silence, parents have a choice. They can go about their business as usual, in the hope that the child will eventually tire of her unrewarding withdrawal and become motivated to join their activities. This keeps sulking and pouting from giving the child power over the whole family. However, the child may withdraw further if she really is unable to make her point in any other way. If the withdrawal seems to have been caused by some slight that needs to be recognized, parents can try slowing down, and being quieter, in an attempt to join in with the child's rhythms and be ready to listen. Either way, don't take brief periods of pouting and sulking too seriously. Instead, encourage your child to use more direct forms of expression to tell you what she feels.

Parents will worry more when a quiet, shy, and sensitive child sulks and pouts. They are aware that she may not have other ways of communicating her distress. When she withdraws into her quiet distant state, you can try to quiet down with her. You might even imitate her mood and her behavior, subtly, and respectfully. As she begins to respond, you can begin to help her. Prepare her gently for transitions. Stand beside her in a new situation, such as school or new people. "I know how difficult this may be for you." Admire her attempts to master her feelings. In this way you are telling her, "I'm here to help you, but I expect you to try, too."

Turning Against a Parent: "I hate you, Mommy!" one 5-year-old shouts, her eyes blazing, her body stiffened, and her hands clenched. Either her mother wilts or she retaliates in the same key; whichever response she chooses, she is covering up her hurt: "How can she say things like that? Does she really hate me?" Next week, if the child dares, she may even say such a thing to her father. Or, more likely, when her father offers to play ball, she may turn her back on him and walk away.

These strong negative feelings come as a surprise to all—the 5-year-old as well as her parents. The father's eyes meets his wife's as if to say: "We've created a monster." Parents wonder what they've done wrong. The child flushes, begins to regret her outburst, but isn't sure how to repair it. Her emotions are surfacing in unexpected ways.

Parents can expect that a child of this age will turn against one parent at a time. A mother may call me to complain about her 6-year-old daughter: "She acts as if she can't hear me, as if I'm not even there. When I ask her to do something, she just walks away. If I reprimand her, she may retaliate with a dirty word. I feel as if I'm losing control over her. As if I'm not even there." Such hostility is even more painful when the child seems closer to the other parent, cuddling and smiling. Then, after a week or two, another phone call: The girl has turned against her father, and suddenly, her mother walks on water.

Just as we saw with younger children, 5- or 6-year-olds are still trying out each parent's role, learning about each—one at a time. The child takes on their mannerisms, their language. As she imitates one parent, she will push that parent away, as if to try out his or her place. This is an aggressive act, and a guilt-ridden one. When parents expect and understand such behavior, they won't have to take it so personally.

Mood Swings and Explosions: Though tantrums are usually less common, violent outbursts of screaming and yelling may become more frequent. Often there is no explanation for them. Sometimes it seems as if the child knows she is soon to face greater responsibilities and demands—kindergarten and first grade, expectations for performance and for self-control. Is she anxious about what lies ahead? Or mourning the loss of the more carefree days of early childhood?

Everyone feels exhausted and confused after these outbursts. Parents are worried: "If it's this bad now, what'll she be like when she's a teenager?" Limits are as necessary and reassuring as ever.

My 6-year-old grandson had just started shrieking at the top of his lungs. He was an out-of-control mess! His mother waded in to try to stop his screaming. As she began to yell at him to stop, he pulled himself together and sedately suggested: "Mom, if you have anything to say, let's discuss it later, when you have yourself under control."

Look behind your child's turmoil. Talk it over with her, and see whether she can tell you that she doesn't like losing control this way. Can she participate in identifying triggers and warning signs for these blow-ups so that she can prevent the outbursts from happening? Can she pay attention to what helps her calm down so that she can come up with ways to cut them short? If she can or will accept your help, ask her to let you remind her of these the next time an explosion menaces.

When a child blows up at a younger sibling, ask her to sit down and collect herself. "Would it help to have a punching bag? You could punch it to let off steam." Or ask for other ideas, a room to scream in, a run around the yard, a ball to slam against the garage door (watch out for windows), and so on.

When her ideas work, commend her. But let her know that sometimes they may not, and that then you'll just need to keep trying. If she can begin to take some responsibility for her loss of control, she will learn a lot about herself. Mood swings and outbursts are as frightening to her as they are to you.

Running Away: A child can't work at pleasing people all the time. She'll still need to try out daring new gestures to see what happens. She must test her parents to see how they'll respond to all the new things she can do. She'll wonder, "Will they stop me now, or won't they?" If they do, she'll be relieved. But she may need to push further still. If she's really angry, or needs to be sure her parents really care, she may "run away," taking her teddy bear or favorite toy with her.

I used to "run away" to my grandparents' house. There, I dreamt about how much my mother was missing me. I was sure she didn't know where I was. That was part of her punishment. I was delivering my message.

Firmness and caring can easily be combined: "Did you really think we would let you do that? Did you really think we wouldn't come after you? You know how much we love you! But you know you can't do this. It's too dangerous. If you are really angry with us, there are other things you can do." Give the child some clay to pound on, or let her draw an angry picture, or make up a story about some mean old monsters that you'll write down for her.

Teasing: (See also *Bullying and Teasing* in Chapter 3.) One 5-year-old asks another, "Are you still sucking your thumb?" Without hesitating, the other replies, "Of course not. I'm not a baby," even though she still does. Just as she knows she shouldn't suck her thumb in public, she is aware of what the wrong answer to a question like this would do to her standing with her peers.

Five-year-olds notice differences and comment on them openly. At first, the awareness of differences raises a child's anxiety. "Why is she different from me? Should I be worried?" "She's bigger than me. She's stronger than me. She's faster than me." Differences such as these call up a child's insecurity. Taunts and teasing are based on such insecurity. By the fifth year, a child learns that she can use them to hurt. "Your skin's dark. You're fat." The other child senses the scorn in the first child's voice and winces. The child who teases feels powerful. Underneath, she may be frightened of the power of teasing, of her own aggression.

How should a parent respond to a child who teases? Look for opportunities that don't hurt others to help her feel stronger, prouder, more powerful. Help her see that to be big and strong she'll have to take on new responsibilities, to use her strength wisely, and to stand up for those who are more vulnerable. Find stories and role models that depict strength and courage in the service of protecting the wrongly attacked and the weak. She can come to see the misuse of power imbalances as "unfair."

Once a child who teases feels more confident about herself, she may be more prepared to consider the teased child's position. A parent can ask, "How would you feel?" Don't be surprised if at first she replies, "I don't care." She may still feel too vulnerable to admit to herself that she does. A parent might simply then say, "Sometimes it may hurt too much to care."

For a small child, it can be overwhelming to think about another child's vulnerability, or about her own responsibility for hurting her. As a parent, it's all too easy to overdo the "lesson," to punish the teasing and miss the chance to help her see the consequences. Perhaps you could help the two children talk out their feelings with each other.

Tattling: When one child reports on another child's "wrongdoing" to a parent, a dilemma arises. Parents can address the tattler's concerns. Tattling will then seem, to the child, to pay off, increasing the likelihood of more tattling. Or, parents can ignore the complaining. The tattler may then be confused about rules and consequences, or worse, be left in a risky situation.

It helps to consider the child's motive for tattling. A child may simply be defending her rights and needs, and unable to arrive at a solution on her own. If this is so, tattling may not be a form of aggression directed at the other child. However, if the tattler is attempting to use your power as an adult authority against the other child, watch out. Her goal may be vengeance, or a way to dominate—important reasons for a parent to stay out of it. Explain that you can't take sides. You appreciate her attention to the rules, but let her know that she'll need to take her concerns back to the other child. You can offer strategies for how the children can work out their differences on their own. You can even role-play various ways that they might talk things over. But in this instance you'll want to turn the job of settling the problem back to the tattler.

Strengthening Conscience: Conscience has dawned and needs reinforcement. Now that the 5- or 6-year-old is aware of her effect on others, she is able to sense the hurt she's caused when she's heedless or cruel. Giving the child a chance to talk about her motives and her feelings provides her with an opportunity to understand herself. This will be necessary if she is to learn to control her aggressive impulses.

When to Worry: A child who is always the brunt of teasing and bullying needs protection—for her safety, and her self-esteem. She is especially vulnerable once she comes to believe that she deserves to be bullied. Adults will need to intervene, for her sake, and for the sake of the teasers and bullies. They too are showing their vulnerability, with their aggressive behavior. (See *Bullying and Teasing* in Chapter 3.)

Other children can often sense when a child is in trouble. If they shun a child, it is usually for a reason. Parents may not be able to recognize the child's problems because they will have adjusted to the child's temperament and behavior. But other children will. When other children shun a child, it should be taken seriously.

At 5 and 6, children may still come to blows as they test their strength, and set up their social pecking order. But very soon they understand who is stronger than whom, and physical fighting wanes. By this age, they should be skillful enough in getting along to avoid major scuffles. If the same 5- or 6-year-old is getting into fights repeatedly, she is letting adults know that something is wrong.

Aggressive acts that are intentionally cruel to a child or an animal must also be faced. A child who is preoccupied with violence, does not show concern when someone is hurt, and feels no remorse when she hurts someone also deserves special attention. A careful evaluation of these concerns by a child psychologist or psychiatrist can help determine what the problem is; among the possibilities are limited social skills, impulse control problems, the raw irritability that goes with depression, exposure to violence, or trauma.

CHAPTER 3

Everyday Opportunities for Mastering Anger and Aggression

Anger

Anger is like fear—an emotional reaction to a threat to our survival. It alerts us to danger, and it pushes us into action: flight for fear, fight for anger. Efforts to stifle anger altogether can be misguided and are bound to fail. In fact, the inability to experience and express anger can leave a child misunderstood, unprotected, even in danger. He may even begin to turn his anger inward.

As the child grows, he will need to control his feelings so that he can figure out the reason for them. He'll have to learn to express his emotional reactions effectively so that others can understand them and will want to respond positively. Most of the time, though, a small child's anger leads to impulsive action, before he has a chance to understand why he's angry, and what to do about it.

The Many Causes of Anger

Some adults may think of anger as an ugly emotion, to be kept at bay at all costs. Yet anger is an unavoidable emotion, and a necessary one. Set off by a variety of different triggers, anger usually serves a purpose for the child. Before determining how to best help a child handle anger, it is important to understand the cause.

Danger and Unmet Needs: The most basic cause for anger is a threat to survival or well-being. Among such threats are pain, hunger, and fear, as well as the perceived risk of being in danger or of being left alone. All these are evident early in life. For example, when a baby screams, parents begin to fall apart. "What is it? I've fed him. I've changed him. What else can I do?" parents wonder, standing over the baby, wringing their hands. He looks up at them. His crying seems to escalate from protest to anger. A piercing, demanding cry: "Why don't you do something?" he seems to be saying.

This earliest kind of anger arises throughout childhood when a need goes unmet. A 5-year-old, suffering from an ear infection, shouted, sobbing, at his father, a doctor, "My ear hurts and *you can't do anything about it!*" His father, as helpless as the child, was, of course, crushed.

Failures: As a child grows older, other causes for anger emerge. One is failure, being unable to accomplish what he sets out to do. An infant can experience failure when he tries to grasp an object he can't quite reach. It's not just that he didn't get what he wanted. He's frustrated because he didn't get the object *for himself.*

Shame and Humiliation: Anger also can arise from the shame and humiliation that can accompany failure. This comes once a child knows what is expected of him and can evaluate his performance to see whether he measures up. A child usually can't quite compare himself to someone else's standard in this way until he is 3 years or older.

One 4-year-old, failing to sort out squares and circles fast enough on a timed test, silently buried his face in his hands. He was ashamed that he'd "failed" the test, but his shame quickly turned into anger aimed at the tester. He ran out of the room and refused any more testing. Can you blame him?

Hurt Feelings: Anger is caused not just by threats to survival, but also by threats to emotional well-being. At first, such threats may be reacted to with anger, but without a clear awareness of the emotions that seem to be under attack. For example, a toddler might have a tantrum when a parent leaves the room. His protest just says, "Don't leave me," without yet being able to explain for himself, or for others, that "I feel all alone."

But as early as 3 years of age, some children have become aware enough of emotional threats to know that someone has "hurt" their "feelings." For children this young, which feelings are hurt? Already, they want to be competent ("I'm good at going to the potty"); to be accepted; and to belong ("She wants me to play with her"). Beliefs such as these—which children need to have about themselves—are vulnerable to attack. Many minor experiences that hurt a child's feelings also can damage self-esteem. "I'm no good" or "Nobody wants me" may seem only a step away from a toilet training accident or a failed play date. To avoid turning anger against himself, a child may need help in readjusting his expectations: "It's okay. Everybody has accidents once in awhile."

Injustice: By 4 or 5 years, a new cause for anger appears. At these ages, children have begun to struggle with the notion of "right" and "wrong." Now, the strongest or pushiest child can no longer always force his way to what he wants. Instead, fairness matters. A child of this age who feels thwarted in his own aims, or hurt and mistreated, is bound to cry out: *"That's not fair."*

A 4-year-old is likely to protest that something isn't fair when he thinks it'll help him get his way. Still, this can be an opportunity to help him think about what fairness really is. "Maybe it's not fair for your little sister to win when she gets a head start. But without it, you know you'll always win because you're bigger. Do you think that's fair?"

Later on, you'll be glad that your child is able to fight for what's fair. Anger need not be reserved solely for one's own threatened self-interests. On the contrary, outrage with injustices suffered by others is a uniquely human emotion. The world needs more adults who have developed a concern for justice and a capacity for outrage. Anger need not lead to rash and impulsive acts if it is followed by careful thought and planning.

More Serious Causes of Anger: When a child seems angry most of the time, when his reactions are out of proportion to the causes of his anger, and when his anger interferes with family, friends, and important activities at school, then his anger may be a symptom of a more serious underlying problem. When a child is depressed, for example, he may seem more angry than sad; he may be irritable most of the day and unable to enjoy activities that once were fun. A child with a disorder that hinders him at school or in making friends—for example, attention deficit hyperactivity disorder (ADHD) or a learning disability—is likely to build up anger that boils over. When there is intense and prolonged anger within a family, as when a marriage is breaking up or domestic violence occurs, a child is also likely to be angry more often, and out of proportion to any immediate trigger.

A parent's reaction to a child's anger may provide another warning sign that professional help is needed. If you find yourself always "walking on eggshells," avoiding conflicts at all costs, or, worse, avoiding the child, then it is time to talk to your child's pediatrician (and perhaps to a mental health specialist).

When Anger Is Thwarted

When anger fails to accomplish its purpose, there are usually five likely outcomes:

1. Anger is acted on, again and again, with increasing intensity, until the child gets what he wants.

2. Anger builds up until he lashes out uncontrollably and his blow up becomes more serious than whatever set the anger off.

3. Bitterness festers. Then, addressing the original cause of the anger may no longer be enough. Instead, revenge becomes the child's goal. For example, anger caused by pain that goes unrelieved for too long may lead to a desire to hurt the person seen as responsible for the pain or who has failed to respond to it. "Payback" may be more or less well-disguised depending on the child's age and level of sophistication. The ways a child tries to hide such urges can be admired—for their cleverness and for the underlying wish to keep angry feelings in check. Passive aggressive retaliation is most likely when a child fears the consequences of a more direct attack on his part.

4. Anger can turn into a grudge. Then, retaliation may take the form of pouting, sulking, and withdrawal, and is directed at the person held responsible for the problem.

5. Anger may not be expressed for fear of upsetting or angering others. The angry feelings may then be turned inwards, leading to self-destructive acts.

All these possibilities should make it easy to see why stifling anger is rarely a solution and why helping a child learn to understand angry feelings and express them effectively is so important.

Helping a Child Handle Anger

Establishing Safety: Whatever the cause, if anger is still exploding, safety is the first concern. Everyone must be assured that they can keep themselves safe, or will receive the help they need to do so. Stop the action. Swoop in decisively: "Stop right now, or I'll have to stop you." Be prepared to show them that you mean what you say. Separating the children involved in a scuffle helps. Isolation gives each of them a chance to calm down and regain control. After they've quieted, give each one a hug. They'll need reassuring that they're still loveable before they'll be ready to listen to your limits.

Setting Limits: Setting clear limits reassures everyone that you will not allow anyone to be hurt. This is critical, because if children are to learn to control their anger, it is important for them not to be too afraid of it to face it. For example, parents may need to say, "It doesn't matter how angry you are. You are not allowed to do that—no matter what."

Soothing and Self-Soothing: At this point, the child will need to settle himself, but he may need your help in accomplishing this. This is when time-outs can help. Don't present them as punishments; if you do, the child will just get all riled up again.

Ways to Help a Child Settle Angry Feelings

- Stopping the action, isolation—leaving the scene: Getting away from the source of the anger can be a critical first step. When a child says, "Don't talk to me" or "Go away" or "Leave me alone," he may be working very hard to isolate himself from whatever is making him angry so that he can get himself under control.
- Soothing—calming efforts: for example, a gentle voice, rocking, a lullaby, a hug. A parent's soothing needs to be carefully timed. A child in the midst of a tantrum needs to be left alone. He's unreachable. Only when it's over will he need and respond to cuddling.
- Self-soothing—one's own calming efforts: for example, thumb-sucking, curling up in a ball, singing to one's self.
- Distraction/diversion: for example, a pleasant thought, noticing something funny, being drawn into an engaging activity.
- Physical activity: for example, pounding a punching bag or a pillow, bouncing a ball or going for a run or a bike ride, even taking a shower or drinking a glass of water.
- Creative expressions: mashing a ball of clay, or pounding on paper with crayons, furiously scribbling, drawing angry monsters or making up stories about them, building tall building block towers and knocking them down, playing out angry scenarios with dolls or puppets.
- "Getting feelings out"—talking with someone who understands can relieve angry feelings. Screaming at the top of one's lungs may or may not.
- New understanding: When a child is ready to talk, help him recognize the other feelings that may underlie the angry ones.

(This is why time-outs sometimes don't work.) Instead, time-outs can be offered as a quiet time for calming down. Suggest deep breaths, a drink of water, a warm, wet wash cloth on the face, a hug. Anger brings a problem to the child's attention, but it doesn't point the child toward finding a good solution. Once the child has settled himself down, he can think more clearly about what is bothering him, and what he can do about it.

Acknowledging Angry Feelings: Sometimes, a few words that show that you do understand the cause of the child's anger, even though you can't accept the aggressive behavior, will help settle the child down. For example, "Of course your friend made you angry when she took your toy. I don't blame you for getting mad at her. But hitting is not the way to let her know."

At first, the child may not want to talk. When a child finally begins to disclose what he's upset about, don't get defensive. What matters, at first, is how important the incident was to him. Don't start off by minimizing: "Of course your teacher didn't mean you are dumb!" Putting things into perspective can come later. For now, ask what the worst thing that happened was, what made him the angriest, or what scared him the most. If a child was angered because no one seemed to know, or listen, or care, telling the story to an attentive parent may be all a child needs to do to let go of it. Later, humor can help too.

Problem Solving: He may need your help to identify the cause of his anger. The relieved look on his face will show you when you've hit on it. Once he knows what has made him so angry, you can help him consider these two approaches:

1. The child can influence others to change, to respond in a different way, or agree to try.
2. He can adapt and respond to others in a different way.

Often, the solution will involve a little of each.

For example, a child who is hungry will need to protest until he is fed. On the other hand, a child who wants candy may have to learn to handle his disappointment. A child in pain will need to make his suffering known until everything that can possibly be done to relieve it has been done. But if it can't be relieved entirely, he will need to learn to put up with it, perhaps by distracting himself, or engaging others to help divert him.

If his anger was caused by some wrong that has not been righted, or some danger that has not been protected against, then a parent will want to find out what the child thinks should be done. The child may, of course, start with the most preposterous recommendations. After having been hit by another child, he may start by suggesting that that child ought to be kicked out of kindergarten forever, or, as one 4-year-old said, "killed until he's so dead he'll never come back." A parent might then respond, "Well that way you sure wouldn't have to worry about him bothering you anymore, would you?"

After the child nods enthusiastically, a parent could then ask, "Do you think there's anything else that could be done that would make you feel better?" If he doesn't respond, you may have to try out a few suggestions (such as talking to the teacher about it, talking it over with the other child, making a plan for what to do the next time), or even to say, "You know, we'll have to come up with some other ideas because we can't really kick him out or kill him."

Lessons Learned: A child who is raised to expect that those around him must always adapt to his needs will be ill-prepared for the world. On the other hand, one who feels he must always give in and never dare advocate for himself will fare no better. Helping an angry child learn problem solving is an opportunity to teach him to adapt to what he must accept and to fight against the unacceptable.

When to Intervene: Are there times when children can be left to work their conflicts out on their own? Rather than rescuing children from their anger, and its consequences, give them a chance—short of seriously injuring someone or themselves—to learn from experience about how far they can go, when they've gone too far. Parents will find it easier to know when to stand back and when to intervene when they know what is reasonable to expect at each developmental stage. (We have described these stages in Chapter 2.) For example, two 2-year-olds tussling over a toy that both want to play with are bound to pull and hit until the more persistent child wins out. What has been learned here? One child will have to face his failed attempt; the other may learn that he isn't entirely happy about getting his way because now he's been abandoned by his friend and must play alone. Or he may not care, yet.

If such scenes are repeated over and over, the same child always dominating, chances for learning wither. It is time to intervene. These become opportunities for practicing sharing, taking turns, putting up with frustration, and beginning to recognize the wishes of others. The children won't master any of this right away. But it's not too soon to work on it.

It will also be worthwhile to intervene when a child is so overcome by his anger that he can neither think straight nor express his anger effectively. He's bound to continue thrashing, and to create angry feelings in everyone around him. Their reactions will only distract him from finding out what has made him so upset. A brief opportunity for isolation to calm himself down can help him save face despite his loss of control. Otherwise, embarrassment can become one more cause for anger to pile on top of anger.

"Use Your Words"

Every day, in childcare centers all over America, 3- and 4-year-olds on the verge of clobbering each other hear this hallowed phrase. To some adults, it is the centerpiece of "emotional literacy"—teaching a child to identify and talk about his feelings instead of resorting to physical aggression. Others see the concept as unrealistic with small children or as culturally bound. What could "use your words" possibly mean to children of this age? It is, in fact, shorthand for a fairly complex sequence of steps.

Children who struggle to understand "use your words" will need the sequence broken down into a series of simpler challenges:

1. A child must stop in the middle of a conflict and hold back on action.
2. He must analyze the situation: "What's going on?" "What am I doing or about to do?"
3. He must ask himself: "What do I want? What am I feeling?"
4. He must then express his feelings.
5. He must become calm enough to listen.
6. Finally, he must be ready to negotiate and find solutions.

Examples, or short lists of possibilities, may also be needed for children younger than 3 years who are still mastering the ability to express themselves with words. They're not yet ready to master this process, but these are ways to help them start learning. The box on page 84 offers a number of questions that an angry child can be asked to think over.

Prevention

Anger cannot always be prevented, nor should it be. As we've seen, it is an inevitable emotion, even a protective one. Anger is sometimes assumed to be dangerous and to be suppressed at all costs. This can make children more frightened of such feelings,

Questions for a Child Who Is Angry

1. What is going on?
   —Are you angry with someone?
   —Are you having trouble sharing or taking turns?
   —Is it that you don't want to do something?

2. How does it feel?
   —unfair?
   —sad?
   —as though you were going to explode?

3. What can you do?
   —"If you hit or kick your friend, how will she feel?"
   —"If you tell her what you want, would she let you have it?"
   —"If she won't, could you offer to share it or trade for something she wants?"

and more alone when they feel angry. They are bound to feel that their anger makes them "bad," and this may make it even more difficult for them to handle such feelings.

Destructive ways of handling anger can be prevented. Children need help understanding their angry feelings even when they also need help accepting that these feelings must not be acted upon. They will need help in learning to experience such feelings without hurting others or themselves. Children will learn from watching others handle strong emotions.

Parents' Anger

Parents can acknowledge when they are angry, explain why, and model ways of expressing anger that are not destructive. This is not always easy. We certainly can't hide our own emotions, but we might hope that they'll go unnoticed by our children. They won't. Instead, without our explanations, children are bound to feel caught up in our angry feelings, and they may even feel responsible.

When our children make us angry, we should let them know—the more directly the better. Sometimes, of course, children can be so infuriating that we may try to silence ourselves to protect them from our rage. And our own rage does need to be reined in before we can figure out how to tell our children what we're feeling and why.

Parents may feel guilty when they react to their children in anger. But children need to learn from the consequences of their actions. If we don't raise our voices and instead speak in sickly sweet tones, they are likely to continue their misbehavior—just to see what happens when parents *really* get angry. A child is far less likely to be damaged by a raised voice than by dishonesty or silent withdrawal. Let them understand why you're angry and what the limits are.

Parents sometimes say to me, "I feel so guilty when I yell at my kids. I can't imagine you ever raising your voice at a child." I must reassure them that of course I do. I explain that a child knows that if he behaves in infuriating ways, anger is what he'll get. When he's irritating, of course my voice will sound irritated—because I am. He'll also learn that my anger or irritation isn't the end of the world, and that sooner or later I'll succeed in getting myself calmed down, too.

Biting

The High Stakes of Biting

Parents of "biters" are frantic. "Where will I leave my child when I have to work?" "Only 18 months old and almost kicked out of school! What will I do with him? What's next?" Parents of a bitten child are also frantic. The broken skin, the purple bruise are too much to take. "How could that child do that? How could the teachers let that happen? Where were they?" And nowadays, teachers worry about the spread of diseases such as AIDS through biting. No wonder everyone goes absolutely wild whenever a child bites. (Although skin infections, treated with antibiotics if necessary, can sometimes occur with a bite that breaks the skin, HIV, fortunately, is not transmitted by biting. That virus is rarely present in saliva, and when it is, it's in too small an amount to lead to infection.)

But there is another reason for such reactions. Biting is frightening to adults because it seems so primitive, almost animal-like. When young children seem to behave like animals, parents instinctively feel it is their duty to "civilize" them. They will be most concerned about behaviors that seem unpredictable, dangerous, and beyond their control.

A Predictable Behavior

In young children, biting is to be expected, and it is rarely dangerous. Parents can't control it. But if they don't overreact, biting will be self-limited, usually stopping before a child is 2 or 2½ years old. Predictably, biting is likely to appear in the first year, often not long after the first teeth emerge. Though adults often associate biting with anger, the first bite may be an exploration of what this new equipment can do, or a passionate gesture of affection. For breastfed babies, the first opportunity is an obvious one.

An Early Communication

Because biting hurts, and because another person's feelings are not immediately understood by the infant, he'll have to bite more to find out what the bitten adult's sudden, intriguing jolts and screeches are all about. It soon becomes a communication. No wonder most children start biting when they possess more teeth than words! One of our colleagues says that, to the 1-year-old, a bite is just the other side of a kiss.

Even later, at 18 or 24 months, a bite rarely seems planned. It occurs when a child is too excited or upset to express himself in any other way. Watch a child of this age bite another. The biter doesn't seem to have intended the reaction he's achieved. Instead, the very first look on his face is surprise. Biting at this age looks far more impulsive—a sudden flood of overwhelming feelings, and a quick release, rather than a hostile or premeditated act.

Overreactions

Does all this mean that biting can be tolerated? Of course not. But by understanding why young children bite, overreactions can be avoided. Usually, children go beyond an occasional chomp and become confirmed biters when adults have reacted frantically. This makes the biting far more exciting than it would otherwise be. Without meaning to, adults can elevate biting from a one-time loss of control to a powerful way of affecting the world. Worst of all, overreactions make the biter believe that he is just that—a biter. He is misunderstood and rejected: No one wants to play with a biter. Left alone, his only hope for human contact—peer interaction or adult attention—is to find another victim to sink his teeth into. A child who is expected to bite, hit, or scratch quickly comes to see himself as "bad." How will he ever expect to find better ways of communicating if no one else believes he can?

How to Handle Biting

When one child bites another, both will need comforting. The bitten child will, of course, need soothing, and attention given to his wound. He'll also need encouragement to stand up for himself, and to insist—when the time is right—on an apology.

As surprising as it may seem, the biter, too, will need soothing. He's bound to have frightened himself with his own out-of-control aggression. Once he's been comforted, he'll feel reassured to hear the limit, and the consequence: "No biting. Ever. You'll have to play by yourself until you can say you're sorry, and keep yourself under control." But try to say this calmly. The biter is the one who is out of control, and he needs to know that you're not.

I used to keep a list of 2-year-old biters so that their mothers could get them together. During these play dates, one toddler would get excited and bite his playmate. The friend would bite back. Both would scream. Through their tears, they'd look at each other in bewilderment, as if to say, "Why'd you do that? You hurt me!" And they'd never bite each other again. They seemed to connect the bites they had given each other with the hurt they'd received: "Did I do that? But I didn't mean to."

Learning to Face Mistakes: Once the biter is calm, he'll have a chance to realize what he's done, especially if the adult can keep his reactions to himself. If the biter does not appear guilt-ridden, he may still be overwhelmed with guilt, and he's probably fighting hard not to feel it, or show it. Reassurance that he can be forgiven and learn better ways of communicating is far more likely to help him accept responsibility for his behavior than loud threats or guilt trips. The latter, on the contrary, are bound to make him blurt out: "I didn't do it!" But if he can't face what he's done yet, he's a step farther away from changing his behavior.

A parent or teacher might say, "I know you feel badly about having hurt your friend. I know you wish you could take it back. You can't. But you can apologize and ask to be forgiven. You know you'll try hard not to bite again. We all know. No one likes to hurt anyone like that." Such expectations for the biter are pressure, but they are also hope for the future.

Learning to Understand Others' Feelings—Empathy: The biter may need help imagining the other child's feelings before he can fully understand what he's done wrong. You may have to say, "See how sad she looks. Do you know why?" He may shake his head sadly. "I think maybe you do. It hurt her when you bit her. And it scared her, too." After a pause, you might add, "I know she likes you very much, and she wants to be your friend. She was so surprised that you would hurt her. Maybe you were, too."

Apologies: The biter will be ready to apologize when he can admit that he feels badly about what he's done. A child who still speaks only a few words at a time may only be able to say so with his big, sad eyes looking into yours as you say it for him. Even older children may have a hard time apologizing. Some will refuse to acknowledge what they've done, or insist that it was the other child's fault. Others will freely admit their responsibility, but stubbornly defy all demands for an apology. They seem to struggle to protect a fragile belief in their own "goodness."

Such children may be helped to apologize with reassurance that they are not "bad," even if what they've done is unacceptable. Still, they may hold out unless there is more pressure, for example, "You'll have to stay right here while the others go out and play unless you can apologize." Such painfully extracted apologies lose most of their meaning. But they are necessary as a way of making your expectations clear.

Forgiveness: After comfort, limits, consequences, and apologies comes forgiveness. Forgiveness is the child's guarantee that there is hope for him to give up biting, get himself under control, find better ways of communicating, and get along with his friends. A child needs to feel such hope if he is to succeed in all of this.

Preparing for the Future: After a biting episode, have a talk with the child about what went wrong. Encourage him to be on the lookout for warning signs. A parent might ask, "Do you know when you start feeling like you're going to bite?" A young child is unlikely to have an answer, but the question pushes him to think, and to wonder. He'll now be interested when you ask, "When you get mad? Or excited? Or can't have what you want?" Next, the child will be ready to hear that biting didn't help with any of these. Finally, other behaviors can be suggested: finding something safe to bite, using words, running around, or asking a grown up for help.

But don't expect this teaching to end biting forever. The next time will be an opportunity to repeat these lessons and to build on them. Don't worry. Biting is rarely seen beyond preschool. Younger children may be surprised and frightened by it, but even slightly older ones look down at it with disdain: "What a baby!" Whatever power a child once found in biting has now been lost—at least for the child who has learned to be sensitive to others.

When Biting Persists

A child who continues to bite beyond the age of 3 or 4 years is likely to have more serious underlying problems, for example, difficulties that interfere with communication, understanding social rules, and impulse control. When a child isn't accepted by his peers, and doesn't know how to behave in ways that are acceptable to them, it is time to pay attention. He'll need the help of a child psychologist or psychiatrist who can clarify the underlying problems as well as help bring the behavior under control.

Bullying and Teasing

Sticks and stones will break my bones, but names will never hurt me.

Is there any truth to this simple rhyme? Perhaps only a little. We teach children to say this to teasers to take power away from them. We'd like to be able to protect them. We want to help them believe that cruel words won't have any effect. But they do. Bullies victimize a child with threats and physical fighting, but teasers can tear down a child's self-esteem, especially once they've learned to aim their taunts at a child's most vulnerable spots.

Bullying and teasing both take a toll. Ask any adult, and he or she is bound to remember, with painful precision, the insults as well as the blows hurled by their childhood peers. Usually, the most readily recalled jeers are those that hit closest to home, closest to the flaws—real or imagined—that as children they'd tried hardest to hide away. The best-remembered fights are the ones that were the most humiliating.

Where It Hurts Most

Often, one child teases another for being "babyish," for displaying a quality or behavior, such as thumbsucking or bedwetting, that is associated with younger children. I still remember when the kids on the back of the school bus teased my friend's sister: "Judy, Judy, doodie-diaper." No one wanted to be caught dead with a dirty diaper. My friend was mortified, and torn between wanting to protect his sister and wanting to pretend he didn't know her. His sister went on to be mercilessly teased for years. He's never gotten over his guilt, and she was loaded down with overwhelming anger well into her adult years. There is a price to pay for teasing.

Children are so motivated to grow up, to shed younger behaviors and replace them with ones that seem older. A child who hasn't learned to hide how much he misses or needs his parents is a compelling target for teasers of 4 or 5 years and older. So is a child who appears weak or defenseless. A "babyish" child's behavior is a disturbing reminder to the teaser that neither child has yet grown up as much as he'd like to believe he has. A bully is especially bothered by this, and will strike out against an immature child as if to reassure himself of how "big and strong" he is with his own brute force.

Facing Differences

Teasing usually begins at around the age of 4 or 5, when children become aware of their differences. At first, differences are intriguing, but hard to understand. To begin to make sense of the differences between themselves and others, children of this age will use their developing ability to make categories: bigger, smaller, weaker, stronger, prettier, uglier, better, or worse.

Early on children will wonder why people are different and whether differences are acceptable. Teasing starts as a first expression of the awareness of these differences, and an early effort to understand what they mean. At this age, children can be given assurance: "All children get teased. When someone teases you, they sure seem mean. But they are interested in you. They are trying to get to know you. They might even be trying to figure out how to be your friend."

One of the first differences that children recognize is gender. So it comes as no surprise that teasing is often related to gender differences. Boys tease girls. Girls tease boys. Each teases his or her own gender for seeming like the other. Underneath the teasing is a question: "Is it okay for me to be the way I am? And to like her the way she is?"

How do children learn to attach judgments to differences? At 4 and 5, they are also learning about right and wrong, good and bad. As they learn to categorize, they're bound to feel that everything must go into one of these categories. They hear the judgments that adults make about differences. Big is "good," and better than small because adults praise children for being "so big." Strong is "good," and better than weak for the same reason.

By 4 or 5 years, children become aware of differences in skin color. But if it weren't for adult prejudices, children would be unlikely to see different skin colors, facial features, or hair textures in positive and negative terms. Children learn racism from the adults around them.

It's not useful to pretend that we're all the same. We're not, and children of this age are just realizing this. Can they understand that we can be equal even though we're different? Rather than telling them what to think, encourage them to think carefully about their assumptions: "Okay. So her eyes *are* different from yours. His skin *is* different from yours. What do *you* think that means?" Give your child a chance to ponder this. Then, you might ask: "How can you tell if someone is a friend? By what they look like? By how they act? By what's on the outside, or what's on the inside?" We may need to think carefully about our own assumptions, too. Children (and adults) may discover that people are not necessarily different or the same in the ways we assume they might be.

When to Intervene

Whether we like it or not, there's little chance of getting through childhood without teasing or being teased. When it is mutual, when children can give and take each others' teasing, it is less likely to be damaging. But when teasing is incessant, with one child always trapped in the victim's role, the other in that of the aggressor, it is time to intervene. Adults will also have to step in when children tease about disabilities, or racial, ethnic, religious, and cultural differences. Forbidding such teasing is only the first step. Helping children to understand what it feels like to be teased and why differences unsettle them is next. Later they can begin to enjoy the excitement that comes with an openness to differences.

Help for the Bullied and the Teased

How can we help a child who is bullied or teased? First, safety must be ensured. Parents will need to find out whether the child is in danger. They may have to escort him to school, and be more of a presence in places such as the playground where the bullying occurs. They may also need to discuss the situation with teachers and other parents.

When a child's immediate safety has been addressed, parents can share the victimized child's feelings with him: "It feels awful when someone is so mean." Talk it out with him. Remind him of his assets. Offer him other ways of looking at himself and his tormentors so that he doesn't have to take the teasing to heart. He can be helped to see that he *does* have power over whether he lets these taunts get under his skin. As my mother used to say, "When other kids tease you, just picture them without their clothes on. But don't tell them—it's your secret weapon!" Taking teasing less seriously may help a child deflect teasing in the future. A child who is bullied may find it helpful to take a self-defense class so that he can project an air of self-confidence that says: "You'd better not try anything with me." Such classes are offered for children as young as 3 or 4 years old. (See *Self-Defense and Martial Arts* in Chapter 3.)

The victims of bullying and teasing can be taught to stand up for themselves, to examine and change the behaviors that seem to single them out for teasing. Opportunities to feel important, strong, and effective will also help these children display an air of confidence that will protect them. Such activities might include traditional ones, such as sports. But if a child can't succeed there, there are so many others—planting a garden, nurturing a wounded animal, helping an elderly grandparent. These children will need help in learning to value and feel proud of their differences so that they can't be used as weapons against them. Parents can help by accepting them as they are and valuing their differences as strengths. Children can fall back on these to protect their self-esteem when under attack.

The child who is repeatedly teased may need help in learning to face his vulnerabilities, and to compensate for them. Often such a child almost seems to set himself up for attack, as if he weren't quite capable of reading his peers' cues and adapting to their social code. Sometimes, he may seem to be crying out "Help—I don't know how to fit in!" One-on-one time with a sensitive peer can help. He'll also need adult support.

Parents of a child who is constantly teased or bullied should talk with teachers to find out how this is handled at school. Although more adult supervision can help, if it conveys the impression that the victimized child is receiving special treatment, it may backfire and lead to more teasing whenever adults aren't around. Teasing and bullying are more effectively addressed when the rules are spelled out and consistently enforced for *all* the children.

If a child continues to be victimized, over and over, he may need a fresh start in a new, more protected peer group. Children who consistently flounder in social situations may have a more serious disorder that interferes with understanding body language and other important but subtle aspects of communication. If you are concerned about this, your pediatrician can refer you to a child psychiatrist, psychologist, and/or a speech and language pathologist.

Help for the Bullies and Teasers

A bully is an insecure, unhappy child. Peers shun him. He is aware of this but does not know how to reach out to friends. He may attack when he feels threatened by signs of vulnerability in another child that remind him of his own. He may use intimidation to keep others from threatening him.

Often an aggressive child has been the victim of aggression. Has he been made to feel small and weak by an older sibling or peer? Is he vaguely aware of his own immaturity—perhaps in the area of language or social skills—and does he seek to compensate by teasing his peers? Bullies and teasers can be helped to feel certain enough of their own competence so they are less threatened by other children's displays of weakness. They can be helped to see their ability to face their own vulnerability as a sign of strength, something to be proud of. But if their bullying persists, damaging their relationships, they, too, may need help from a child mental health specialist.

Hitting, Kicking, and Scratching

Most children go through a period of hitting, kicking, and scratching in the second year. It usually begins sometime around a child's first birthday. Parents are often the first victims.

Why Does a Child Attack?

For a child, parents are the first source of comfort and sustenance, so when something goes wrong, of course they're the first to be blamed. Yet, when a child is about 7 or 8 months old, parents will find themselves pressed into denying or frustrating his new demands. At that age, he can express his wants more clearly, begin to get around on his own, and try to do things he can't. Be ready for him to take his frustration out on you! By around 9 months, he has also learned how to test a limit. He'll try it out to see whether you always mean what you say. When the answer is "No!" he's bound to fall apart and lash out. Suddenly, without thinking, he'll scratch his fingernails across your face. What a shock!

How to Help

Unfortunately, your surprised reaction is likely to confuse him. To understand what's going on, and regain control of the situation, he'll scratch you again. He's checking to see whether your response becomes more predictable. It's time for you to teach him not to hurt you.

Make a stern face, and just as sternly say, "No. Don't hit. It hurts." But don't get too excited, or he'll think it's a game and want to try again and again. Put him down, or turn away from him.

Parents' first task is to stay in control themselves. Take your own time out if you need to: You are his first model for self-control. He may make you so angry that you want to smack him. Don't. He needs you to model for him what he must learn.

Hitting, kicking, and scratching are also a last resort for children when the demands of a social situation exceed their social skills or their ability to use words to express themselves. They may also hit when they feel belittled, or when they want to assert their dominance in a schoolyard pecking order or with their siblings. When a child feels frightened and without protection, for example, if the adults around him use physical aggression, or threaten to, he may become physically aggressive himself. If your child singles himself out with repeated fighting with peers, talk to his teacher and his pediatrician. They can help you find specialists (speech and language pathologist, psychologist) to look into these possibilities.

Learning to Get Along

Sometimes preschool children just collide into each other, get hurt, lose control, and then flail back in retaliation. They're still learning to balance, to plan out the way they'll move, but they can't always anticipate the results. They'll also attack when they want to play with a toy made more exciting by the child who is already using it; when they want their turn now, not later; when they are losing but want to win. Preschool children hit, kick, and scratch because they are still working on important skills:

- making friends
- paying attention to other people's needs
- sharing
- taking turns
- losing gracefully
- apologizing, and meaning it
- negotiating relationships
- resolving conflicts, solving problems
- anticipating, understanding, and caring about the feelings of others

When adults stop to consider how much preschoolers have to learn, it becomes easier to see why they still often resort to simpler and blunter tools. How many adults still haven't mastered these? The second and third years are the appropriate times for children to begin to learn these social skills.

Your Seven-Step Response to
Hitting, Kicking, and Scratching

1. *Stop the fighting, reestablish safety:* "Stop hitting right now." If the children don't respond at once, separate them. Send them to separate rooms if they try to go at it again. Safety and containment come first.

2. *Comfort the victim, and the attacker:* Both the "victim" and the "attacker" need to be comforted. Strong feelings between them—hurt, fear, guilt, or a longing for revenge—will make it harder for each child to face what has happened and repair their relationship.

3. *Clear limits:* After comfort come clear limits. Limits establish the safety that is necessary to face the "crisis" and to begin to learn from it. "It's wrong to hit, and it won't be allowed." Say it like you mean it, and make sure you look like you do. Be sure, too, that other adults around back you up.

4. *Consequences:* Now, children will be ready for consequences. These are needed to teach them how to connect their actions with the results. "If you hit someone else like that, you'll have to stay by yourself until you're ready to play without hitting. I can't let anybody get hurt. And I can't let you hit." There are also the natural consequences of such behavior: "If you hurt people, they won't want to play with you. And they won't want to be your friend." This is a lot for a young child to learn. Consequences will help him understand.

5. *Lessons learned:* After comfort, safety, limits, and consequences are established, look for the lessons that each new conflict can teach. Parents and teachers need to consider

continues on next page

Your Seven-Step Response to Hitting, Kicking, and Scratching
continued from previous page

each situation carefully. What was the challenge? What was the missing skill? How can the children be helped to learn it? For example, when one child accidentally hurts another, help the "victim" to think clearly about his attacker's intentions: "Do you really think he meant to hurt you? Should we find out if he feels sorry that he did?"

6. *Empathy:* When one child grabs a toy from another, help the grabber step into the other child's shoes: "Can you imagine how you would feel if someone grabbed a toy away from you? How do you think she felt when you took it from her?" It will be easier for children to think about these important questions if they are asked with more patience than exasperation.

   The other child may also need help learning to care about the grabber's feelings. A parent might say, "Of course you don't want to share a toy that you're having so much fun with. But that little boy, watching all your fun, will want to play too. He shouldn't grab. But if you tell him that he can use your toy when you're done, or if you share it, then maybe he won't have to grab."

7. *Conflict resolution:* After understanding each other's feelings, the children may be ready for conflict resolution. To the grabber, a parent can say, "You'll need to give it back. And say you're sorry. But you could ask her to let you play with it when she's finished. Or you could ask her to trade it with one of your toys."

Ghosts from the Nursery

The aggressive behavior of young children is unlikely to cause serious harm. Our response to it, though, is critical. Such behavior can stir up parents' memories of the past, or worries for the future. These can prevent them from reacting appropriately to what is happening in the present.

Memories of being bullied as a child, or of guilty feelings for having been a bully, are bound to arise. Parents who were bullied themselves may have trouble setting limits on their child's attacks. Some parents seem to take excessive pride in their children's aggressiveness. Of course, a child's feistiness should be valued, but not his ability to dominate others physically. If parents tolerate harm to another child, they are sending a dangerous signal.

Parents can't help but wonder how their children will "turn out," and they often look to their children's behavior as a prediction for the future. If an adult relative is out of control, parents are bound to wonder, "Will my child turn out like him?" For people whose families have been ripped apart by violence, either within their families or around them, the fighting of young children is bound to be especially frightening. For parents who know that they must prepare their children to defend themselves in a dangerous world, handling such early conflicts takes on even greater urgency.

For example, one parent raising an energetic, dark-skinned young boy told me, "Twenty-five percent of African American males spend some time in prison. If you're a young black man, all you have to do is be in the wrong place at the wrong time. I have to be sure my boy learns to stay in control. If he loses it once, he may not have another chance. Other people's kids just need to learn to stay out of trouble. We have to teach ours to run from it!" No wonder the innocent kicking and hitting of young children who have not yet learned better ways of communicating and asserting themselves can be so distressing for parents. The stakes are so high! These early years are the best opportunity to help children work on self-control, empathy, and knowing right from wrong.

Self-Defense and Martial Arts

It's a terrible feeling for a child to think that if he's threatened he'll just have to give in. Some parents teach their children to strike back if attacked; others hesitate to say it's okay, even in the context of self-defense. Yet, without permission and skill to protect himself, a child has no choice but to become a victim. But a child who feels fully secure in his ability to stand up for himself, and is empowered to do so, is less likely to be involved in fights, either as the instigator or as the victim.

Sometimes parents whose children have been teased or beaten up may goad them into fighting back, but for revenge rather than for self-protection. When reserved for the right occasions, however, self-defense skills can be reassuring and protective. Martial arts classes can be one way for children to master these skills and to know when it is appropriate to use them.

Martial arts classes for children, when carefully conducted, teach children about the true meaning of self-defense and how they can identify situations in which fighting back is justified. Such classes can also give children the kind of confidence that bullies can sense and are scared off by. Often a child's best way to prevent being attacked is to peacefully convey the confident expectation that "no one messes with me and gets away with it." Girls, in particular, can benefit from self-defense classes that help them believe that they need not be victims. The more well-prepared children are to defend themselves, the less often they will find it necessary to use these skills.

If you are considering a martial arts class for your child, be sure that you choose one that teaches self-defense. Aikido, "the way of harmony," is the least violent of martial arts and it focuses on self-defense. Other less violent martial arts that stress self-defense (for example, immobilizing techniques rather than striking) include Judo, "the way of gentleness," and Jujitsu, "the technique of gentleness." Classes adapted for children as young as 4 years old are available. For children this young, the classes should emphasize

- awareness of surroundings and safety
- verbal skills to avoid aggression

and when the child is threatened:

- being clear and direct about saying no with words and body language
- running away and telling the right adult

Avoid other martial arts (for example kick-boxing and Aikijitsu—which use throws, joint locks, pressure points, and striking) that emphasize aggressive fighting rather than self-defense. Be sure, too, that the instructor is properly trained, and that the facilities meet safety requirements so that risk of injury is lessened.

Sports and Aggression

Ours is a sports-oriented culture. As early as age 3 and 4, children are introduced to basic sports skills such as throwing and catching. By 6 or 7, those who haven't mastered these and others may already feel left behind, and left out, too. Because our mainstream culture values competition, first graders will know who's the best and who's the worst at sports in their class. Catching up can already seem like a hopeless task. Yet, when practicing these skills means extra time with a parent, a child is bound to feel heartened—as long as the focus is on having fun rather than on perfection. Parents will need to take care that their eagerness doesn't backfire and become more pressure for the child.

Why does competence in sports matter? For boys, still more than for girls, the pecking order in sports mirrors a broader one that establishes who rules on the playground and who must be ready to give in. Although sports can be a relatively safe way of harnessing children's physical energy and aggressive urges, they can also reinforce relationships based on the power imbalances among them.

Boys admire sports prowess in their peers—even boys who see themselves as inferior in this area. It is the rare child who can distance himself from the values of his peers to affirm his own strengths in a different realm. By 8 or 9 years, sports prowess becomes a major factor in determining a boy's popularity. Boys who find themselves at the bottom of the sports skill ladder are likely to be rejected socially. They can suffer damage to their self-esteem and, without support from adults, may even be predisposed to more serious problems, such as anxiety and depression.

More Ghosts from the Nursery

The importance of early sports experiences is easy to deduce from parents' recollections of their own athletic exploits. These will fuel their hopes for their children's sports prowess, and their worries. A parent remembers whether he was routinely picked first or last for a team, whether he hit grand slams, or whether he always struck out.

Some parents, anxious for their children to succeed in sports as well as socially, start them off early and give them hours of deliberate practice that risk taking the fun out of the game. These parents sometimes seem to take winning more seriously than their children, who are caught up in playing the game. Children know that sports should be fun. From the sidelines, parents shout "Go get 'em." Whose aggression is this?

Other parents, who felt hopeless as young athletes, may push their children to compensate or try to protect their children by steering them toward less competitive activities or pastimes they will be sure to excel at. If their children do not show athletic interest or ability, parents can set up alternative activities, for example, art, music, chess, woodworking, or environmental and nature programs. Children involved in these activities can find an accepting peer group. They may need some gentle help from their parents to believe that their special group's values (for example cooperation, or creativity, as opposed to competition or physical prowess) are important.

Whether a child is a gifted athlete or always the last one picked, sports bring out differences that we must help our children accept and face. Rather than smooth them over, why not be honest about such differences? Then our job is to help our children accept each other and themselves. This, of course, will be easier for our children if they can be sure that their self-acceptance is far more important to us as parents than their performance in sports.

Learning to Play by the Rules

An early challenge for children is to understand the rules of the game, and that the rules apply equally to everyone, no matter how much everyone wants to win.

Learning to Win and to Lose

Children younger than 4 years are often only vaguely interested in winning. They are usually much more taken with the process—of chasing after a ball, or of trying to figure out where to go next—than with the end result. But by 4 and 5 years, when children are becoming aware of the differences between them, winning and losing take on new meaning. The "winners" and "losers" draw attention for their differences: "Who's the strongest? Who's the wimpiest?" are questions children ask now.

At 5 and 6 years, children are more aware of their limitations. As a result, being the best, and winning, is a valued way of making up for such difficult-to-face realities.

Losing, though, is another reality that is hard to face. Young children are bound to deny it, shrieking "We won, we won!" even if they didn't. When the sad reality of losing can no longer be denied, they're likely to dissolve into a puddle of tears. Or they may explode and attack the winners: "You cheated! That's why you won!"

How to Help Your Child Learn Good Sportsmanship

Although it is important to understand why children feel strongly about winning and losing, and why they react the way they do, parents need to be clear about their expectations. Lying and cheating are understandable, but they are not acceptable. Being a sore loser is not something that anyone can admire or feel proud of.

Firm expectations may need to be accompanied by face-saving maneuvers. Losers may need their parents' help in mastering their feelings of discouragement and humiliation. But first, they may need help just to get themselves under control. Pat reassurances—"You were great!" or "Don't worry, next time you can win!"—are liable to backfire at this point. Help them face their disappointment and even the anger they feel toward themselves: "How do you think you did?"

If the child blurts out: "I *stunk!*" parents may be alarmed. But the child is pulling himself out of his dejection by sharing such feelings with them. A parent might reply, "It sure feels terrible to lose, especially when you try so hard." As the child's sadness begins to subside, a parent might add, "It really mattered to you a whole lot, didn't it?"

Now the child will know that he is really understood. He may be ready to have some help in stepping back, taking perspective: "Do you think that you'll be able to have another try when you play again?" The child may be ready to value how hard he tried, even if he didn't win. But perhaps most important is the clear message that winning or losing is the child's issue, not the parents'. If you've been too involved, your child will know and will feel even more disheartened. You'll need to admit it if you've added to the pressure, and to apologize.

Learning to Play as a Team

A special challenge of team sports is learning to share the glory and the blame. It's a struggle for children of any age to keep

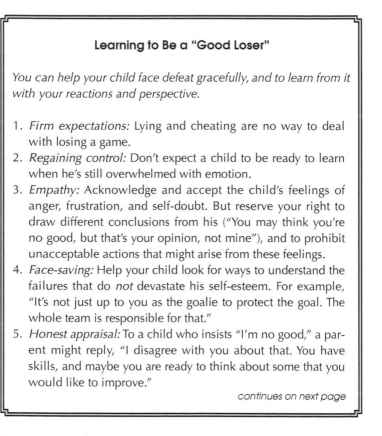

Learning to Be a "Good Loser"

You can help your child face defeat gracefully, and to learn from it with your reactions and perspective.

1. *Firm expectations:* Lying and cheating are no way to deal with losing a game.
2. *Regaining control:* Don't expect a child to be ready to learn when he's still overwhelmed with emotion.
3. *Empathy:* Acknowledge and accept the child's feelings of anger, frustration, and self-doubt. But reserve your right to draw different conclusions from his ("You may think you're no good, but that's your opinion, not mine"), and to prohibit unacceptable actions that might arise from these feelings.
4. *Face-saving:* Help your child look for ways to understand the failures that do *not* devastate his self-esteem. For example, "It's not just up to you as the goalie to protect the goal. The whole team is responsible for that."
5. *Honest appraisal:* To a child who insists "I'm no good," a parent might reply, "I disagree with you about that. You have skills, and maybe you are ready to think about some that you would like to improve."

continues on next page

from venting frustration against team mates and instead to focus on encouragement. When the team loses, it's tempting to protect one's own self-esteem by singling out others to hold responsible. Children's abilities are bound to vary enough for everyone to see when one or two of the children really couldn't

Learning to Be a "Good Loser"

continued from previous page

6. *Taking perspective:* At first, the moment of defeat can seem like the end of the world. But eventually it is forgotten. You can help your child become aware of how these first reactions gradually shift. At the next defeat, you can remind him of his observation.
7. *Encouragement:* Reassure your child that he can get back on track. Let him know that he needn't be so hard on himself: "It's hard to keep trying when you feel so discouraged. But if you keep on trying, you'll feel better."
8. *Turning it back to the child:* Your child needs to know that handling defeat is his job, not yours. So is pulling himself together again so that he can face the next challenge.
9. *Final reminder:* Whether your child wins or loses, the point of the game is to have fun.

live up to the demands. Then, even children who don't want to hurt other's feelings are caught in the dilemma. "Do we tell the truth, or pretend that we all stunk?"

Parents can help children handle their frustration without hurting the other kids. After a soccer defeat, for example, some children may want to kick the ball—as hard as they can—at the goal, over and over, until they're spent. Others will collapse into silliness, chasing after each other, tumbling on the ground. Let them. But if they gang up on a team mate, let them know that they are exhibiting poor sportsmanship: "Sure everyone's upset about losing. But we're a team and we've got to stick together. That's part of playing the game." Sadly, many coaches and parents make such lessons take a back seat to winning—for younger and younger children.

Team mates may be able to see that tearing down a player's self-confidence will only hurt their game. Coaches and parents can model the importance of focusing on the positives, on hopes for the next time. The adults may have to look hard for positives to praise in the less-skillful child. For that child, effort and commitment may be the winning qualities. Young "stars" may also need help with their shortcomings—for example, hogging the ball or poor teamwork. The best athletes may also need to work on calming themselves down after making a mistake so that they can learn from it. Coaches and parents can privately offer individual children (the stragglers and the stars) a chance to practice needed skills. Perhaps a sensitive team mate to partner with in practice might help as well.

Playing Dirty

When children play dirty–an unnoticed trip or push, for example—winning has taken on more importance for them than playing the game. Often, they are responding to pressure from parents and coaches. Some coaches even teach children in elementary school how to foul the other team's players in ways that the referee will be unlikely to spot! With such mixed messages, playing dirty is to be expected.

There should, of course, be no tolerance for playing dirty—it's wrong, and it's dangerous! Unfortunately, playing dirty—that is, breaking rules that are meant to insure fairness and everyone's safety—is found all too often in the adult world. Children are outraged at those who play dirty—and they're right! Can we help them find effective ways to respond? They may need our support to say: "I'm not playing with you anymore. Playing dirty takes the fun out of it."

When Children Fight: Sometimes, playing dirty degenerates into a brawl. One child, overheated, on the edge, and truly desperate to win a soccer match, takes a shot at the goal. Suddenly, he's thrown off balance by someone from the other team who's given him a deliberate nudge. Beside himself, the first child lunges at the second, throws him to the ground, and begins pummeling him—completely out of control. Isn't there something about the pressure of competitive team sports that is likely to bring children close to this edge? Besides, isn't this what often happens in professional hockey games? Our children will need better role models if we are to help them handle their disappointment and anger without blowing their tops!

When Adults Fight: Things become even more confusing when the adults at children's sports events begin to fight. Parents scream at the children on both teams. They shout at the coaches. The coaches shout at each other. Everyone shouts at the referee. How can we expect children to handle their intensely aggressive

---

Sample Rules and
Consequences for Children's Team Sports

1. Players may not trip or push. They will be warned, and then punished.
2. Children who fight on the field will be thrown out of the game.
3. Serious offenses will lead the player to be "benched" for the rest of the season, and, for the worst violations, banned from the league.
4. Parents are not permitted to shout the names of players, nor to yell advice or specific comments about individual players.
5. They may not address players on either team in a negative way. Only general words of encouragement are permitted for either team, for example, *"Go, team!"* or *"Good job, team!"*
6. There shall be no arguing with the referee—ever, by anybody, including parents and coaches. The game will be played as the referee calls it.

Children will model on adults as they attempt to abide by these rules and keep their own strong feelings under control.

---

feelings effectively if the adults are completely out of control? Perhaps these parents do not realize that their children are watching and taking it all in as a model for their own behavior.

With carefully explained rules, firm expectations, and consistently upheld consequences, athletics can offer opportunities for children (and adults) to master their aggressive urges.

Children (and parents) need rules to guide their behavior, especially at predictable times of tension and conflict. Rules that permit competitive team sports to proceed fairly, and without explosive violence, carry a broader message. These are a major opportunity for children to learn and care about the basic principles that we all need to uphold if we are to live proudly and peacefully with each other. Sports offer opportunities to learn anger management and the values of good sportsmanship.

Tantrums and Self-Control

Tantrums are universal. And yet they are so disturbing to parents. Here are three reasons why:

1. They always seem to happen at the most inconvenient and embarrassing times and places. This is what makes tantrums so dreaded, and so *powerful.*
2. In the midst of a tantrum, a child, at least one under 3 years, seems so completely out of control. To some parents, the child may even seem possessed, powerless. The child parents thought they knew seems to have vanished, the reasoning part gone.
3. A child older than 2½ or 3 years may seem to use tantrums as a threat, and as a tool to get his way. When this happens, he may try everything else first. He'll even seem to give you one last warning look before he hurls himself

on the floor. Even then, he seems maddeningly aware of his audience, slowing up every now and then to see whether you're still there, and raging louder than ever if you try to intervene.

This is when parents will need to realize that their *power over a tantrum lies in giving up power,* and letting the child learn to control himself: "I can see you're out of control. And I know you'll be able to get yourself under control, by yourself. I'll just stay out of your way until you've settled down."

Anatomy of a Tantrum

Tantrums begin with a trigger—either internal or external. Identifying such triggers is key to avoiding future tantrums. Then there is the build-up, which may be a gradual thundering rumble, offering chances to stave off the storm, or as fast as a flash of lightning, too fast to be prevented. At the peak of a tantrum, all control appears to be lost.

In this state, there is no thinking, no reasoning, no communicating. There is only an explosive discharge of tension. This is certainly a physical experience as well: Skin turns red and clammy, heart rate and breathing quicken, and the child's body flails or becomes convulsed with uncontrollable sobbing. After the worst is over, the clouds scatter and the child begins to subside, gathering himself little by little. But the child is still fragile in these first moments, and he is easily overwhelmed by an intrusion into his efforts to soothe himself.

Only later can the child be comforted. With more time, he can participate in reviewing what has happened in the hope of avoiding it in the future. Before he can do this, though, he'll need to be commended for bringing himself back under control, and given reassurance that he can master these frightening tantrums. A hug will help him feel safe again.

What Causes Tantrums

Tantrums are likely to appear sometime around the first birthday. Initially, they may be more likely to be brought out by hunger, fatigue, boredom, or too much stimulation, though these may also cause tantrums in older children.

From 18 to 36 months is a typical time for tantrums. Children of this age are so readily overtaken by intense feelings. To add to their challenge, they now want to make their own decisions, but they are often torn between one temptation and its opposite: "Do I want to or don't I? Will I or won't I?"

Tantrums are also likely to be set off when a child reaches beyond his current abilities to try for something that he just isn't ready to succeed at. They can be the price of a new step in development that the child is about to take—a touchpoint. At each age, of course, there will be a different set of challenges that are just out of reach. A child who can't quite crawl or walk may fall apart because he can't stand the frustration of not going where he wants to go. A slightly older child may throw a tantrum as he tries and fails at a fine motor task, such as putting together a puzzle. A child who is not yet able to talk, but is flooded with important thoughts and wishes that he needs to express, may also melt into a puddle of tearful, inarticulate rage. Trying to get along with peers is also likely to lead to tantrums early on. Unable to assert themselves effectively and unable to see when they need to compromise, young children can overwhelm each other, and then explode.

Tantrums occur because children, already faced with a wide range of challenges—motor, cognitive, emotional, communicative, and social—are lacking skills they will need to deal with all of these. Beyond limited coordination, fine motor movements, or words is the lack of several basic abilities—frustration tolerance, self-soothing, patience, among others—without which tantrums are fairly inevitable.

These are skills that take time to emerge. As they do, the child will have more capacity to manage his frustration, his decision making, and his self-control. In the meantime, parents and teachers can model these skills with their own behavior. They can also seize "teachable moments," the tense situations that are tantrums in the making, to work on helping the child find ways to soothe himself and tolerate frustration.

Tantrums are also likely to surface when a child is under stress. In addition to the developmental "stress" of a touchpoint, a child is bound to fall back on tantrums at other times of major change, for example, when a new baby is introduced into the family. An older child may throw a tantrum just when a younger sibling has his first one!

How to Prevent a Tantrum

In addition to anticipating the situations and challenges that are likely to set off a tantrum, such as those we've just mentioned, adults can help children anticipate them. Then, they can be prepared to avert predictable tantrums.

Before going to the store, for example, parents can discuss with children the temptation of the candy at the checkout counter. They can make it clear that buying sweets will not be a solution and then encourage the child to plan other ways of getting himself through the store owner's greedy challenge to every child of his age.

They may have to help the child come up with some new ideas: "You could keep your eyes closed until we're through. I'll hold your hand. Or you could help me empty the grocery cart and try not to pay attention to the candy racks. Or you could bring your teddy bear and hug him when he's sad about no candy." One parent even offered to put away the money not spent on candy bars to save up for a toy.

Tantrum prevention also requires careful observation of the warning signs—in the child and in yourself. Most parents know when a child is beginning to lose control—his voice is a pitch higher, and he may stumble over his words. His face reddens, the muscles in his neck stand out, he breathes faster, he wrings his hands.

The worse tantrums have been, or the more inconvenient and embarrassing a tantrum would be, the more tense a parent becomes. This can add to the child's tension. If parents see the child's warning signs and can brace themselves, they'll be better able to help a child catch himself and learn to calm down—before it's too late.

To settle a child down before the tantrum takes over, consider first the cause. If a child is hungry, tired, bored, or overstimulated, your best chance at averting the crisis may be to attend to these needs if you possibly can. If you can't, you might still be able to encourage him to work on soothing such feelings himself. A favorite stuffed animal or soft blanket to stroke and cuddle, or a quiet song to sing, can help at times like these.

If, however, a child is frustrated because he wants something that he can't have, you don't have to give in. If you do, you'll be making tantrums more likely next time. A child needs to know that his tantrums are not so powerful, nor so scary, that you can't stand up to him. He needs the reassurance that you can dare to brave his anger, that you can look out for him even when he can't, and that you can protect him—from himself.

Instead of giving in, you have choices. You can try to comfort him. You can try to distract him. Distraction often is effective with toddlers, which is fortunate because you won't be able to reason with them. But these may just prolong the tantrum. If so, pull back and wait. When it's over, cuddle him and reassure him that he'll learn to get himself under control. With an older child, commiseration and empathy helps. Instead of getting angry with him for wanting something he knows he can't have, let him know that, even though you can't let him have what he wants, you can see why he wants it and that you understand why he feels upset. He'll be less frightened of feelings like these if you can understand them and accept them: "I know how much you want to get candy every time we go to the store. It's so hard to see all that stuff and not be able to get it."

One way a child masters tantrums is to model on parents' strategies for self-control. When you are overwhelmed by frustration, anger, or disappointment, turn this into an opportunity to show your child effective ways of handling such feelings. For example, when someone cuts in front of you at the dry cleaners, you might say, "That lady was so rude I felt like smacking her. But I didn't. I just said to myself 'Damn that lady,' and thought about how you and I could talk about it. And then I felt better." Don't try this, though, until the lady is out of earshot.

Later, try to talk over what happened. Be careful not to embarrass him. Start with his strengths: "You were so mad, but you did such a good job of calming yourself down. It was really hard, wasn't it? But you did it." Then, help him look for the lesson in what went wrong. Can he learn about what sets him off, what to avoid, how to prepare himself for predictable frustrations and disappointments? Can he identify the things he can do (for example, asking for help, trying to compromise, recognizing that he can't always have his way, changing the subject) or that you might do (for example, reminding him of his ways of soothing himself) to help him calm down before he explodes?

How to Handle a Tantrum

- If a child can safely be left where he is when in the midst of his tantrum, leave him there. Back off. If he is using his tantrum to communicate something to you, walking away is the clearest way to show him that he'll have to find a better way of telling you what's on his mind.

- Before you step back, reassure him matter-of-factly that you know he can settle himself and that you'll reconnect when he's finished. But don't say too much. It's his job to get himself under control. Leaving it up to him is a sign of respect, your way of showing that you know he can do it. You could, though, quietly hand him his favorite stuffed animal or blanket to soothe himself with.

- If you can't leave him where he is, for example in a store, or on a sidewalk, scoop him up. Some children find it comforting to be held when they are having a tantrum, and will gradually subside if they feel your firm and persistent hold. Once you have him in a safe place, paying no attention is your best approach.

- Usually, though, it is best to stay out of it. But if you must restrain a small child in order to keep him out of danger, these maneuvers can help: Put the child on your lap, facing away from you. Put your arms around his to keep them still and clasp your hands over his belly. If he's kicking, put one of your legs over both of his, lightly scissoring them against your other leg, so that he can't hurt you. Take care, of course, not to hurt him.

continues on next page

How to Handle a Tantrum
continued from previous page

- If he's butting his head, or trying to bite you, hold both his arms with your right arm, put your left hand firmly against his left cheek and gently press his head against yours, with his right cheek against your left cheek. Explain to him, quietly, that you will hold him until he settles down, so that he doesn't get hurt and so that no one else does, either. Rock him a little, or even hum quietly. Gradually, you'll feel his body relax, and his breathing slow down.
- If your child grows even more frantic when being held during a tantrum, move him as quickly as possible to a safer place (for example, from the store to your parked car, where you can sit quietly with him—don't leave him alone there). Say as little as possible, except to let him know that nothing is going to happen until he's settled himself.
- If the child keeps reaching out to you, or coming to you before he's calm, give him time. Don't let him engage you yet. The "silent treatment" may make him wilder, so briefly let him know that you'll talk together when you're sure he's finished and can stay calm. If you try to talk over the incident with him while he's still worked up, to make your point or to let him plead his case, he's likely to fall apart again. Let him know: "We'll talk about this when you're able to without getting upset."

Don't expect this blow up to be the last, and don't let him get discouraged when he has another.

If your response to your child's meltdown gives him the impression that he can expect to get his way if he throws a tantrum, he is bound to repeat the behavior, over and over, even beyond the age by which he should have outgrown tantrums. Instead, he needs to know that temper tantrums represent his loss of control, not an increase in control over you.

If you feel your child does have more control over you than he should, he will probably pick up on this, and be frightened. Children need to know you're in control, especially when they're not. Remember, your child doesn't like having tantrums anymore than you do. They can be frightening and embarrassing.

When to Worry

Tantrums are common in children under the age of 4 or 5 years. Most often they are limited to a period of several months between 18 and 36 months. Typically, each tantrum lasts no more than fifteen or twenty minutes. Most of the time, it should be fairly easy to identify the trigger, or at least the conditions (fatigue, hunger, frustration) that make a child vulnerable to a tantrum.

Some children, though, may have more frequent tantrums that last a half an hour or longer. They may also be unusually intense, with flailing limbs, and blood-curdling shrieks. The child may seem out of reach and unaware of the world around him. When it's over, the child may appear exhausted, and even fall asleep. He may not remember much about the tantrum. An evaluation by a qualified child psychiatrist or psychologist would be in order for a child who has frequent tantrums like these. Some children who have tantrums such as these are thought to have a childhood version of bipolar disorder. Because certain uncommon neurological disorders can also cause sudden violent outbursts, a neurological evaluation might also be called for.

Some children—whose tantrums do not appear to have a readily identifiable trigger—may be hypersensitive to touch or sound or even sight, and they may fall apart when they are over-stimulated. Once this is understood, they and those around them can look out for and avoid these triggers, and find ways to handle them when they can't. Other children may blow up over seemingly trivial triggers when their speech development is delayed. Parents can ask their pediatrician for a consultation with a speech therapist.

Children with ADHD or a learning disability often must deal with more frustration than most children; as a result, they may be more likely to have tantrums. Children with anxiety or phobias may fall apart when they are overwhelmed with worries, or when they find themselves forced to face a fear that they are unprepared for.

Another reason for seemingly unprovoked tantrums is depression. Even young children can suffer from depression, which can make them intensely angry, irritable, and easily pushed over the edge. They may seem angry or gloomy most of the time, and they rarely seem to find pleasure in anything.

Among other possible causes of unusually frequent, long-lasting, or intense tantrums, is trauma. Young children who have been physically or sexually abused, or who have witnessed domestic violence, may not be able to tell anyone about this in any other way. Usually, though, they'll have other symptoms as well: fearfulness, recurrent nightmares, sexual preoccupations or sexualized behavior, distress at bedtime and with changing clothes, problems with using the bathroom, and so on. If you are concerned that your child's tantrums may not be normal, you deserve to have your concerns attended to. Start with your pediatrician, who may refer you to a child psychiatrist or psychologist.

Television, Videos, and Computer Games

Television

After a rash of bloody schoolyard massacres committed by students in the United States, TV and video game violence came under attack as among the likely causes. Some in the television industry—making their arguments on TV news programs—claimed that there was no evidence of a link between what children watched on TV and their behavior. Yet during the preceding 30 years, study after study had already demonstrated that young children, and older ones, exposed to videotaped aggression were more likely to behave aggressively.

According to an American Academy of Pediatrics report, only 18 of 3,500 studies on the association between media violence and violent behavior have failed to show that a relationship exists. This report points out that the correlation is stronger than other generally accepted ones, including the link between secondhand smoke and lung cancer. One study, for example, found that 5.7 percent of adolescents who watched less than one hour of television a day committed violent acts in later years, compared to 28.8 percent of those who watched for three or more hours a day. Children who witness media violence have also been shown to be desensitized to violence, yet at the same time they see their world as a more dangerous, frightening place.

These findings are especially alarming because 68 percent of infants and toddlers spend more than two hours a day looking at television or computer screens. Young children watch, on average, four hours of television per day. They witness many thousands of violent acts on television each year, since 60 percent of TV programming includes violence, and an average hour of TV portrays from three to five violent events.

Television and the media are the biggest competitors for our children's hearts and minds. Clearly, we cannot entrust our children's well-being or their future to the television industry. Nor can we hand over the remote controller to our children before we have taught them not to believe everything they see, before we have instilled in them the values of our own traditions.

Children often think that to be accepted by their friends they must watch the same shows their friends watch. Many believe that to keep up with their playmates they must have the latest action figure or doll. Often, the products marketed by playing on such insecurities can, like television itself, interfere with children's health and well-being. Soda pop, candy, and other unhealthy foods are obvious examples. So are elaborate toy machine guns, grenades, tanks, grotesquely muscle-bound action figures, or sexualized clothing, jewelry, and make-up.

Limiting TV Time: Families will need to turn away from commercial culture to their own family relationships if they are to protect their children from such influences. Parents are a child's most important model, and the longer the TV stays off, the more impact they will have. Parents who use the time they have together with their children to talk, sing, play, just hang out, or even argue, rather than watch TV, will have a chance at transmitting their ideas, traditions, and values.

TV time should not be used as a reward. It makes it seem more valuable than it is. For the same reason, don't take away TV watching as a punishment—unless your child breaks your rules about what and how much to watch. When that happens, the punishment fits the misbehavior: "No more TV today if you can't turn the TV off when I tell you to."

The American Academy of Pediatrics recommends that children watch no more than an hour of television per day (even more caution is recommended for children under the age of 2) and that televisions and computers never be placed in a child's room. In addition, we suggest you keep televisions out of the kitchen and other rooms where the family regularly gathers. Don't let TV become a member of your family, even if you do watch it. If you leave it on all day just for company, consider music instead. It's less likely to distract a child from more important activities.

Don't bother with a big, expensive, flat-screen TV and special speakers placed all over the room. A small TV will do. (Radiation may be a concern with older TV sets.) Don't bother with satellite dishes. The worse the reception, the less your child will want to watch. The bigger and better the sound and image, the more intensely your child is likely to be affected by whatever televised violence you are unable to protect him from. The less attractive your television is, the less you'll have to struggle with your child about watching it.

Choosing Shows to Watch: Your child need not watch TV at all; but if he does, choose carefully. Some shows for young children are free of violence and help them to understand angry feelings and the effects of aggression on others. Look for shows like these. Or shows that will open your child up to new people, places, and ideas and teach him to enjoy the differences between himself and others. Stay away from programs punctuated by commercials; these are designed to make your child think he needs something he doesn't have and to encourage him to nag you into buying whatever is advertised. Advertisers do not necessarily share your goal of helping your child learn and grow.

Watching Together: Watching television with your child is your chance to be sure you know exactly what he is watching and how he reacts to it. It is an opportunity to teach him to question and to think critically. Young children often won't know the difference between reality and fantasy. Believing in fantasy is a privilege, and a necessity of childhood. But when children's fantasies (for example, "to be big and strong") are used by ad agencies to market sugary cereals or elaborate war toys, a child's inability to tell the difference is being exploited. Then parents will want to help a child wonder: "Is that real, or not?"

Slightly older children may need help in sorting through the violence they see on television. Questions such as "Do you think he meant to hurt that lady? Did he have any other choices? Was he right? What should happen to people who do things like that?" can help children learn to *think* about what they see, rather than fear it, or copy it.

Older children will be ready to learn to ask other questions: "Why would they show someone killing someone on TV? Why do people want to watch it? Why do they make commercials? Do they tell the truth or do they just want us to buy things?" Children who learn to stop and think before they *react* are also learning to stop and think before they *act*—an important step in preventing them from hurting others or being hurt themselves.

Some parents argue that the world is a violent place and that their children had best be ready for it. But TV violence is unlikely to teach children how to challenge violence and protect themselves against it. Children are still struggling to understand and control their own angry and aggressive feelings. Sensa-

---

TV-Proofing Your Child

- Avoid television for children younger than 2 years.
- For children older than 2 years, permit no more than an hour a day of TV.
- Carefully select violence-free programs.
- Watch TV with your child so that you can talk over the difference between fantasy and reality; you can also help older children ask critical questions about what they see.
- Offer alternative activities, for example, board games, cards, puzzles, singing and dancing, sports.
- Do not permit TV or computer screens in children's bedrooms.
- Stay away from big, fancy TV sets.
- Don't use TV watching as a reward or a punishment.
- If no one's watching the TV, turn it off.
- Remember that your child is modeling his TV watching habits on yours.

---

tional, glorified television violence is bound to make them more afraid and confused.

Children can learn about anger and aggression from fairy tales and children's stories such as Maurice Sendak's *Where the Wild Things Are*. Stories read aloud are far less overwhelming than televised images. They can be slowed down to leave room for a child's questions and reactions. The fantasies in story books are easier to distinguish from reality than television shows are, and a child can take in the lessons the stories teach without being quite so frightened. Fairy tales can be scary. But these books can be a less overwhelming way of facing violence together because they address the predictable fears of childhood. Reading them together is a chance for fears to be shared. Pretending that fears and aggression don't exist by avoiding them altogether leaves a child all alone to grapple with them. You might also encourage your child to make up his own fairy tales so that he'll have a sense of control. (See *Books for Children* in the *Bibliography.*)

Video and Computer Games

Video and computer games are different. Television asks only for a child's passive attention, but video games require his utmost concentration. The TV-viewing child lazes back limply on a couch. But the young video game enthusiast sits on the edge of his chair, or stands, twisting his whole body as he pulls and jerks on the joystick to simulate the blast of a machine gun, the detonation of a grenade, or a simple low-tech kick in the face or ribs of a street-fighting opponent. With every direct hit, there is a fiery flash, the sound of spurting blood as it appears to drip down the screen, or simply a ding-ding-ding and more points for every deadly shot.

There are some nonviolent video games. But since Pac Man first made its debut a few decades ago, video games have become increasingly violent. Street-fighting scenes, complete with sexualized images of men and women kicking and slashing each other, have become commonplace. Other games put the young player behind the barrel of a gun and reward his rapid reflexes with a blood-covered screen as brains and intestines burst out of his victim's bodies.

Though children everywhere in the United States play games like these, the nation was shocked when one of the teenage schoolyard killers at Columbine was reported as saying to his sidekick just after he had shot a classmate, "Look at his brains spill out on the desk!" Perhaps parents who buy their children video and computer games would do well to try them out first themselves.

There is a simple way to protect children against the effects of violent video and computer games: Don't buy them. Even so, your children will probably encounter them at friends' houses. You'll still have to help them learn to question such games, what they teach, and the motives of those who make and sell them. Don't lecture. Instead, ask probing questions. Learning to think critically will help prevent your children from being sucked in by the powerful attractions of such games.

Don't make a big deal about keeping them out of your house. Forbidden fruit is bound to taste sweeter. You might simply say, "We have other things to spend our money on. You'll have more than enough chances to try out this stuff at other kids' houses." There are plenty of video and computer games that are not based on fighting and killing; some even manage to be exciting while teaching useful skills and knowledge. Steer your child toward a variety of games like these and then let him choose the one that he's most intrigued by. Play it with him to make it even more appealing.

Some computer and video games allow children to play and to learn to work together. Don't let solitary ones take too much time away from play with friends. Children can really learn to handle aggression and angry feelings only when they have a chance to experience them and to practice managing them in social contexts.

The American Academy of Pediatrics recommends an "electronic media-free environment" for children's bedrooms. If older children need a computer in their rooms for homework, don't hook it up to the Internet. They can share your computer for the Internet research they need to do for school. You can click on "History" to check on the sites they've visited. You can also install software that allows you to control their Web surfing.

Music

Younger and younger children are listening to the violent and graphically sexual lyrics of rap and heavy metal music. Many also watch the equally graphic videos that accompany these. Adults are shocked to witness a 4- or 5-year-old repeat perfectly the words and gestures of such music. The lyrics' heroes rarely pay for their "crimes." Usually, these go unpunished. In the songs, the heroes present themselves as role models and give all kinds of justifications for their violent acts.

Television's power comes from the direct effects of visual images on the brain, but music uses sounds and rhythms to capture attention and play on emotions. Both can stimulate the emotional centers of the brain, bypassing those that provide judgment, insight, reason, and impulse control. This is even more likely for young children, in whom these abilities are far less developed.

There is another source for the power that television and violent lyrics exert on young children: the perception of social acceptability and desirability. At younger and younger ages, children are being led to believe that watching gruesome scenes on television proves their bravery to friends; by the same token, listening to "teenage" music establishes their "maturity."

Children learn the values that will guide their behavior from the adults around them. Yet on our radios they may hear lyrics that celebrate murder and rape, or that revel in more subtle exploitation of the weak by the strong, or of women by men. Some will be frightened at first. Some may feel more powerful when they can identify with the bravado and posturing of these songs. Other children know that such actions are wrong, and not to be modeled on. Yet they are drawn to these opportunities to "be bad"—just by listening, or singing along. Certainly children crave chances to test and even to break their parents' rules. But a steady diet of violent lyrics will numb children to their real-life implications.

What can parents do? Don't listen to this music, or at least not in your child's presence. Don't let young children have radios in their rooms. As a child grows older and is bound to hear violent and sexually explicit music in all too many places, talk with him about it. Don't start out by judging. Instead, listen. "Do you like it? What do you like about it?" If a child answers, "I like the beat," ask: "What do you think about the words?" Find out whether he understands them, and how. Then, encourage him to question the behaviors the words describe and the motives behind them. Help him see the victim's perspective: "How would you feel if someone treated your little sister that way? Your mother?" Let him know that most people find swearing and obscenities offensive, and will think less of him for using such language. (See "Swearing and Toilet Talk" in *Discipline: The Brazelton Way* by Brazelton and Sparrow.)

Some parents may try to shut out such influences altogether. We wish it were possible. But short of moving to a desert island, it probably isn't and parents may do best to teach their children how to protect themselves by becoming critical thinkers. Soon enough, you won't always be present to control what your child hears and sees. But early on, you can give him the skills to question, and the values against which to measure whatever he is exposed to.

Toy Guns, Action Figures, and Other Aggressive Toys and Games

Some parents insist, "I'll never buy my child a toy gun. I don't believe in war and I don't want him to learn about it." What does a toy gun have to do with war? What is a child really expressing?

Watch a 5-year-old boy play with his friends. Whether toy guns are off limits or not, sooner or later, they'll point an index finger at each other, cock back their thumbs, and blast air out of their mouths as they pull the imaginary triggers. What are they doing? Using their imaginations. Playing. Do they really want to kill anyone? No. Of course not. But they are trying out common and compelling feelings.

Why do these parents feel so strongly opposed to toy guns? Of course, committed pacifists may want to forbid them. However, taboo toy guns may then take on an additional glow of forbidden fascination. For some parents, there seem to be other reasons.

Just take a look at the almost exclusively male action figures that children of this age also are so fascinated with. They are, of course, overtly sexual representations of pumped-up stereotypical maleness. The fascination 4- and 5-year-olds have with such anatomical detail has not escaped toy manufacturers. Children of this age know now how small, vulnerable, and dependent they are on their parents. It's no wonder that they're drawn to handguns and other macho symbols of power—not to kill, but to be big and strong. It's also understandable for parents to react strongly to such wishes.

A less obvious concern underlying some parents' opposition to toy guns is their own discomfort with aggressive feelings. Such feelings, often accompanied by a swaggering bravado in boys, are present in all children at this age. Forbidding such toys won't make these feelings go away. On the contrary, children will manufacture their own toy guns—with sticks, empty paper towel rolls, or their own fingers—so that they can play out and master their aggressive feelings. We might do better to let them make their own weapons rather than buy ready-made ones. This way, they can be creative, use their imaginations, and explore their own fantasies instead of playing out those of the adults who design increasingly elaborate (and expensive) toy weapons.

Many parents find it difficult to face aggression in young children as a natural and inevitable feeling. Forbidding opportunities to try out these feelings in play is likely to heighten a child's interest, and even intensify the play. But if parents can let their children explore these feelings safely through play-fighting and learn to identify and talk about them, their children will be better prepared to master such feelings.

Witnessing Aggression

Children have always had to face aggression in the world around them. But now they face new kinds of aggression—some never seen before. And it is often magnified and brought into our homes by the high-tech games they play, and in the news media's bids for our attention. Our children are at risk for fearfulness, desensitization, a shift in values, and expectations for a dangerous world. Can we help them believe in the possibility of a more peaceful one?

A young child's first concern about aggression in the world is for his own safety: "Will I be okay?" His second is for his care-givers' well-being: "Will my parents be alright? Will they still be able to take care of me?" The closer conflict is to home, the greater the impact. This is why domestic violence is so devastating to a child. A young child first learns about aggression in his own home.

Parents' Conflicts
Children watch their parents' struggles with careful attention. They become used to predictable parental arguments. They learn to buffer themselves from the inevitable conflicts. They may try to defuse them, or offer their own "bad" behavior to divert parents from their quarrels. They often even learn how to turn parents' disagreements to their own short-term advantage. In the long run, though, parents who allow a child to play one off against the other will find themselves unable to exert the authority that children need if they are to feel secure and to thrive.

Marital discord becomes damaging when children fear that their safety or their parents' is threatened, or that they may lose a parent who threatens to leave. When arguments lead to frightening physical violence, or when it is in the air, but unspoken and unexplained, children are put at risk.

If parental conflicts are unavoidable, how can parents protect their children from its effects? First, avoid involving them in matters that are not their affair. This is more easily said than done, especially when one or both spouses are fired up. But you can establish ground rules and *try* to stick to them. For example, if the children are present when a disagreement sparks, parents can agree to put off the argument. They can schedule time when they can talk things over in private.

Sometimes it can be reassuring, and an opportunity for modeling, to acknowledge the disagreement and your plan for handling it: "We're going to talk about this ourselves later. We'll figure it out. We can take care of it. It's not your issue." Don't be surprised if they hear you when you think they can't. Expect them to be listening hard for your arguing. They are likely to worry, and to feel responsible for the outcome. Children today see divorce all around them. Each time parents fight, their children may wonder, "Are my parents going to get divorced now too?"

Your children will usually know when you've argued. And they'll need some explanation. Simply acknowledge that "I know you can tell that Mommy and I are angry with each other right now. Sometimes we disagree with each other and get mad. But we'll talk it over, and try to make things better." (Don't, though, give false reassurances, for example, if you're actually on the verge of separation. Their trust in you is too valuable.)

The children may even need to know what parents are fighting over. Otherwise, they will assume that they themselves are the source of the conflict. But when you share such information, don't offer it in a way that invites them to take sides. Parents might say, "You know we fight about who forgot to get gas, or silly things like who forgot to put the cap back on the toothpaste." But don't say which parent always leaves the cap off. And don't encourage them to decide which one of you is right.

If your arguments are so intense that you can't tone them down or postpone the worst for times when the children are safely out of earshot, then you deserve to get professional help for your relationship. Whether you can learn to turn your destructive fights into constructive ones, ones that you learn from, or whether you must come to grips with the end of your relationship (no matter hard you have worked at it), your children will benefit from the clarity you gain. In such circumstances, you may both find it useful to remember that the only person you can ever really change is yourself.

War and Terrorism

In the months after the terrorist attacks of September 11, 2001, preschoolers and kindergartners all over the United States added new activities to their play. Suddenly, paper airplanes were everywhere, and children hurled crayon missiles at them to knock them out of the air. Building-block towers were going up faster and higher than ever, only to be vigorously smashed down. Action figures became pilots and flight attendants and terrorists.

Had these children become more violent, mirroring the heightened violence in the world around them? Probably not. Instead, it seems more likely that they were using play to explore and master their fears, to imagine themselves strong enough to stay safe in a world where the adults seemed to have failed them. Even within the *relative* safety outside war zones, children are learning to hate, to harbor fears they cannot handle. Political factions and the media prey upon our fears and our children's. Images, often distorted, of helpless parents and children are used to polarize warring factions.

How can we expect our children to handle their own conflicts peaceably when grown ups don't seem to know how? War is hard for any of us to understand. How can we possibly explain it to our children? First, we must listen to their questions, and then try to understand what images of war might mean to them. We may be surprised.

Shortly after the U.S. invasion in Iraq, a 4-year-old came up to me with huge eyes and asked: "Dr. B., why are we fighting a war with a rock?" I had to answer "I don't know." He seemed comforted by our shared question even though I didn't have an answer.

Of course, we'd like to think that young children don't know about war and don't need to know. But even infants are exquisitely sensitive to their parents' emotions. They may not know that a war is on, but they can't help but be aware of their parents' preoccupations. Sadly, some infants and children are affected more directly, when, for example, one or both parents are mobilized and sent away; or worse, when one is injured or killed. We learned of more than one breastfeeding mother who, after losing her husband in the World Trade Center terrorist attacks, also lost her milk.

Children's questions and reactions will differ with age. For infants and young children, the main concern is their own safety and that of their parents and caregivers. Sadly, we can't always reassure them of this. Still, though, we can let them know that we will do everything in our power to protect them.

Children who are 2 or 3 years old will ask why: "Why do these people have to fight like that?" They're not likely to fully grasp the seriousness of war. They still imagine that harm can be undone, and that people can wake up from death as they do from sleep. The simplicity of young children's questions makes them among the most important that any of us will try to answer. Yet how can we begin to respond when we ourselves barely understand?

Rather than offering simple answers that teach hatred and reinforce tendencies to see the world in black-and-white, we can share our children's uncertainty and confusion. A parent might say, "I don't know why they fight like that. It doesn't make much sense, does it? Why would people want to hurt each other?" We can also share their most obvious natural responses: "I wish we could make them stop."

Children of 3, 4, and 5, in their struggle to understand why, are likely to blame themselves. This is because they see so much of what happens around them as the result of their own actions, thoughts, and feelings. For example, a child can easily misinterpret the loud claps of thunder as an expression of his own anger, or as punishment for some recent misdeed. Though a child of this age is unlikely to tell us so, he is at risk of thinking that acts of war or terrorism happen because "I was bad."

Pat reassurances are unlikely to help unless a parent first explores a child's thinking. Instead of starting with "Of course it's not your fault," it may be more helpful to say, "Tell me why you think that." Then, if a child can talk about what he has done wrong, or what he thinks is bad about himself, he can be helped to see that this is not connected to the world's woes. "I know you feel badly about punching your little sister. And you know you mustn't. But how do you think those people with the bombs could even know about it?"

Watch as the child begins to look up with relief before going on to ask, "And do you really think they would blow up all those people because of what *you* did?" Then, the child might ask, "But why were they so mad?" A parent might answer, "I don't know. Probably for things a lot worse than you punching your sister. Maybe because their houses and land were taken away, or because their entire families were killed. But no one has the right to do anything like that, no matter how mad he is."

When a young child feels responsible for the harm that befalls others, especially if they are close at hand, he can seem to take the weight of the world onto his shoulders. This is especially likely when a parent or close relative has been hurt, or just seems to the child to be sad, anxious, or preoccupied. The child may become angry and sullen. You can see that he takes it personally. Or he may suddenly become interested in nurturing others, especially those who seem vulnerable. Parents may be touched by his wish to take in and nurse a stray dog or a bird with a broken wing. They will also do well to evaluate the burdens the child may be bearing. (Such a nurturing reaction is a wonderful one, but don't count on it.)

At the ages of 4, 5, and 6, children will also begin to ask about fairness. They will wonder about whether an act of aggression can be justified as self-defense or to "get even." At these ages, they can be asked to consider whether two wrongs make a right, or whether turning one's cheek is best. Most likely, though, children of this age will resolve such moral dilemmas practically. Safety, avoiding harm, and not getting caught are usually still their main preoccupations.

By now, children are more realistic about their own limitations. Grandiose fantasies of 2- and 3-year-olds to "make the whole world all better" are bound to give way to more practical and seemingly selfish ones. It is understandable that children who are aware of how vulnerable they are will focus on their own well-being. Parents may be able to gently nudge children into thinking beyond themselves by honoring such realistic concerns.

More than ever before, detailed news of violence comes to us instantly from the most distant lands. Such news, disturbing as it is, burdens us with a new responsibility, a new challenge—to care. Even as adults we are overwhelmed. We can retreat into apathy and hopelessness. And so can our children. We can turn off the TV news, and for young children we certainly should. (See *Television, Videos, and Computer Games.*) But trying to protect them from it altogether will leave them unprepared for the rude awakening to come. We can help them learn about our world at a pace they can handle. We can help them hold onto their need to care by helping them find small things they can do—raising money (with a lemonade stand or a bake sale) for food and medicine, collecting old books or toys to send abroad, and writing letters to newspapers and politicians.

Bibliography

Books for Parents

Bok, Sissel. *Mayhem: Violence as Public Entertainment* Cambridge, Mass.: Perseus, 1998.

Brazelton, T. B. *Touchpoints: Your Child's Behavioral and Emotional Development.* Cambridge, Mass.: Addison Wesley, 1992.

Brazelton, T. B., and J. D. Sparrow. *Discipline: The Brazelton Way.* Cambridge, Mass.: Perseus, 2003.

_____. *Sleep: The Brazelton Way.* Cambridge, Mass.: Perseus, 2003.

_____. *Toilet Training: The Brazelton Way.* Cambridge, Mass.: Da Capo, 2004.

_____. *Touchpoints 3–6: Your Child's Behavioral and Emotional Development.* Cambridge, Mass.: Perseus, 2001.

_____. *Understanding Sibling Rivalry: The Brazelton Way.* Cambridge, Mass.: Da Capo, 2005.

Canada, Geoffrey. *Fist, Stick, Knife, Gun.* Boston: Beacon Press.

Goleman, Daniel. *Emotional Intelligence.* New York: Bantam Books, 1995.

Greene, Ross. *The Explosive Child.* New York: Harper Collins, 2001.

Greenspan, Stanley. *Growth of the Mind.* Cambridge, Mass.: Perseus, 1997.

Haddon, Mark. *The Curious Incident of the Dog in the Night-Time.* New York: Random House, 2003.

Hannibal, Mary. *Good Parenting Through Your Divorce.* New York: Marlowe & Co., 2002.

Hetherrington, Mavis, and John Kelly. *For Better or for Worse: Divorce Reconsidered.* New York: W. W. Norton & Co., 2002.

Johnson, Robert, and Paulette Stanford. *Strength for Their Journey: Five Essential Disciplines African American Parents Must Teach Their Children and Teens.* New York: Broadway Books, 2002.

Kindlon, Dan, and Michael Thompson. *Raising Cain: Protecting the Emotional Life of Boys.* New York: Ballantine, 1999.

Linn, Susan. *Consuming Kids: The Hostile Takeover of Childhood.* New York: New Press, 2004.

Schiraldi, Glenn, and Melissa Hallmark Kerr. *The Anger Management Sourcebook.* New York: McGraw Hill, 2002.

Schor, Juliet. *Born to Buy: The Commercialized Child and the New Consumer Culture.* New York: Scribner, 2004.

Thompson, Michael. *Best Friends, Worst Enemies.* New York: Random House, 2001.

Books for Children

Bang, Molly. *When Sophie Gets Angry—Really, Really Angry.* New York: Blue Sky Press, 1999.

Donaldson, Julia, and Axel Scheffler. *The Gruffalo.* New York: Dial, 1999.

Gantos, Jack. *Rotten Ralph*. Boston: Houghton Mifflin, 1980.

Harris, Robie. *It's So Amazing: A Book About Eggs, Sperm, Birth, Babies, and Families*. Cambridge, Mass.: Candlewick, 1999.

Kellogg, Steven. *Much Bigger Than Martin*. New York: Puffin, 1992.

Lasky, Kathryn. *The Tantrum*. New York: Macmillan, 1993.

McCloskey, Robert. *One Morning in Maine*. New York: Puffin, 1976.

Sendak, Maurice. *In the Night Kitchen*. New York: Harper Collins, 1996.

_____. *Where the Wild Things Are*. New York: Harper Collins, 1988.

Dr. Seuss. *My Many Colored Days*. New York: Knopf, 1996.

_____. *The Sneetches and Other Stories*. New York: Random House, 1961.

_____. *Yertle the Turtle and Other Stories*. New York: Random House, 1958.

Silverstein, Shel. *The Giving Tree*. New York: Harper Collins, 1964.

Steig, William. *Spinky Sulks*. New York: Farrar, Strauss, and Giroux, 1988.

Van Allsburg, Chris. *The Polar Express*. Boston: Houghton Mifflin, 1985.

Viorst, Judith. *Alexander and the Terrible, Horrible, No Good, Very Bad Day*. New York: Macmillan, 1972.

Books for Professionals

Bandura, Albert. *Social Learning and Personality Development*. New York: Holt, Rinehart & Winston, 1975.

Gabarino, James. *No Place to Be a Child: Growing Up in a War Zone*. San Francisco: Jossey Bass, 1998.

Gilligan, Carol. *In a Different Voice.* Cambridge, Mass.: Harvard University Press, 1982.

Kreidler, William. *Creative Conflict Resolution: More Than 200 Activities for Keeping Peace in the Classroom.* Parsippany, N.J.: Goodyear Publishers, 1984.

Newman, Katherine S. *The Social Roots of School Shootings.* New York: Basic Books, 2004.

Salovey, James, and John Mayer. "Emotional Intelligence." *Imagination, Cognition, and Personality,* vol. 9 (1990).

Stern, Daniel. *The Interpersonal World of the Infant.* New York: Basic Books, 2000.

Thompson, Michael, and Catherine O'Neill Grace. *Best Friends, Worst Enemies: Understanding the Social Lives of Children.* New York: Ballantine, 2001.

Web Sites

For workshops for young children and their parents on learning about anger:

Family Communications at www.familycommunications.org.

Mr. Rogers' Neighborhood, "Parents & Teachers" at www.pbskids.org /rogers/parentsteachers.

On childhood aggression and the media:

Children Now at www.childrennow.org.

Georgetown University Children and Media Project at www.cdmc .georgetown.edu.

The Sesame Workshop at www.sesameworkshop.org.
The TV Project at www.tvp.org.

For information on self-defense classes for children 3 years old and older:
www.impactboston.com links to sites across the United States.

Videotapes

Rudavsky, Oren. *Hiding and Seeking: Faith and Tolerance After the Holocaust.* 2004.

Shapiro, Justine, and B. Z. Goldberg. *Promises.*

> *Promises* follows the journey of a filmmaker who travels to Jerusalem and the West Bank and meets seven Palestinian and Israeli children. A beautiful and deeply moving film, *Promises* moves the conflict out of politics and into the realm of the human. For more information and to order the film, visit www.promisesproject.org.

Touchpoints: Your Child's Behavioral and Emotional Development: A Three-Part Series by T. B. Brazelton. Available from the Brazelton Touchpoints Center at www.touchpoints.org.

Index

About the Authors

T. Berry Brazelton, M.D., founder of the Child Development Unit at Children's Hospital Boston, is Clinical Professor of Pediatrics Emeritus at Harvard Medical School. His many important and popular books include the internationally best-selling *Touchpoints* and *Infants and Mothers.* A practicing pediatrician and leading advocate for children for more than forty-five years, Dr. Brazelton has also created the Brazelton Touchpoints Project (www.touchpoints.org) to support child development training for healthcare and educational professionals around the world.

Joshua D. Sparrow, M.D., is Assistant Professor of Psychiatry at Harvard Medical School and Special Initiatives Director at the Brazelton Touchpoints Center. He is the co-author, with Dr. Brazelton, of *Touchpoints 3–6,* and the *Brazelton Way* series on *Calming Your Fussy Baby; Discipline; Feeding Your Child; Understanding Sibling Rivalry; Sleep;* and *Toilet Training.*